Stitch of Courage

Stitch of Courage

Courage

A Woman's Fight for Freedom

Linda K. Hubalek

Aurora, Colorado / Lindsborg, Kansas

Stitch of Courage
© 1996 by Linda K. Hubalek

Printed in the United States of America

For details and order blanks for the *Butter in the Well* series and the *Trail of Thread* series, please see page 107 in the back of this book. If you wish to contact the publisher or author, please address to Book Kansas!/Butterfield Books, PO Box 407, Lindsborg, KS 67456. Each book is $9.95, plus $3.00 s/h for the first book ordered and $.50 for each additional book.

Consulting Editor: Dianne Russell
Cover Design: Jody Chapel, Cover to Cover Design
Cover photo of Maggie Kennedy, circa 1880
Maps and photos courtesy of Ivan Pieratt and Linda K. Hubalek
Quilt design used on cover: Sawtooth Star

Publisher's Cataloging in Publication
(Prepared by Quality Books Inc.)

Hubalek, Linda K.
Stitch of courage : a woman's fight for freedom / Linda K. Hubalek.
p. cm. -- (Trail of thread ; 3)
Includes bibliographical references.
SUMMARY : Tells the story of a young woman living in the new state of Kansas during the Civil War.
Preassigned LCCN: 96-83117
ISBN 1-886652-08-2
1. Frontier and pioneer life--Juvenile fiction. 2. Kansas--History--Juvenile fiction. 3. United States--History--Civil War, 1861-1865--Juvenile fiction. I. Title. II. Series.
PZ7.H833Sti 1996   813'.54
                              QB196-40264

To the women in and behind the battle lines:
Your courage to fight gave freedom to more
lives than you will ever know.

"The ladies of Lawrence were brave and plucky," he confided to someone before he left, "but the men . . . were a pack of cowards."

—William C. Quantrill, quoted in
History of the State of Kansas, 1883

Her youth had been passed in the stormiest period of Kansas history. She had seen men shot down before her eyes; she had witnessed and suffered from the raids of border ruffians, had known what it was to have her father in daily danger of his life, had lived for years in a section that saw war as no other in our land had yet seen it and as few have since . . .

—*War Talks in Kansas*, 1906

Books by Linda K. Hubalek

Butter in the Well
Prärieblomman
Egg Gravy
Looking Back
Trail of Thread
Thimble of Soil
Stitch of Courage

Acknowledgments

I would like to express my sincerest thanks to all the family members, researchers, and librarians who helped with *Stitch of Courage*. Thank you for making the whole *Trail of Thread* series come alive for me and for my readers.

Linda Katherine Johnson Hubalek

Table of Contents

1861 Connection of Main Characters

Kennedy Sisters

Mary Ann Kennedy Liming, age 36

Caroline Kennedy Perkins, age 23

both live in Ohio

Maggie Kennedy, age 15

moved from Ohio to Kansas in 1858

future sisters-in-law

Pieratt Sisters

Sarah Pieratt, age 13

George Ann Pieratt, age 11

Emma Pieratt, age 8

*moved from Kentucky to
Kanas in 1854*

Maggie's brother's wife

Shields Sisters

Nancy Shields Pieratt, age 31 ⇐ Pieratt sisters' stepmother

Lucinda Shields Kennedy, age 22

*both live in Douglas Co., Kansas,
came from Illinois in 1855*

Jane Shields, age 29

Elizabeth Shields, age 24

Martha Shields, age 20

Rachel Shields, age 16

*other sisters living in Illinois
or Shawnee Co., Kansas*

Stitch of Courage

While researching for this last book in the *Trail of Thread* series, my main question was, How did the women survive the battles and hardships caused by the war?

We think the Civil War took place in the South, but the plains states endured their share of battles and tragedy. The Kansas and Missouri feud over slavery flared up during the war because of the raiding carried out by both factions. Even though Missouri stayed with the Union, it also kept its slaves. This caused Kansas Jayhawkers, under the protection of the Union uniform, to raid bordering Missouri counties to free the slaves, often returning with the looted belongings of the slaveholders. These men wanted a reason to retaliate against Missouri for its raids on Kansas when it was trying to become a free state; the Civil War was the perfect excuse.

Missouri guerrillas avenged the Kansas raids by terrorizing Kansas border towns. This vicious circle climaxed with the raid on Lawrence, Kansas, on August 21, 1863 by William Quantrill and his 450 followers. Interview accounts say the town's destruction was worse than the battlefield at Gettysburg.

But the war did not end in Kansas and Missouri with that blow. In the fall of 1864, the Confederates and guerrilla sympathizers raged across Missouri one more time, heading for the Kansas border. By martial law, all able Kansas men were called out to defend their state. Farms were left unattended, businesses closed, and towns were empty of the menfolk. The women waited at home, knowing that their men were standing on the state line, outnumbered by the vast Confederate Army headed their way.

Think of the horrors these women witnessed. They were truly caught in the middle. They didn't know where their men were fighting, or even if they were alive. They had to feed their families, and keep the farms and businesses going while their providers and protectors were away. In many cases their husbands were murdered, their belongings plundered, and their houses burned, right before their eyes.

I began the *Trail of Thread* series with Deborah Pieratt, who traveled from Kentucky to the territory of Kansas in 1854.

Margaret Ralston Kennedy's battle for survival in the second book, *Thimble of Soil*, showed how women had to endure the clashes of the free-state and proslavery supporters as the fate of the state was decided. This book also linked two neighboring families together, one from the North, the other from the South.

Then the Civil War started, which is where I start this third book. *Stitch of Courage* tells the story of the orphaned Maggie Kennedy, who followed her brothers to Kansas in the late 1850s. She was the niece of Margaret Ralston Kennedy and married James Monroe Pieratt, son of Deborah Pieratt. As a young woman, and arriving in the state at the end of the period known as Bleeding Kansas, she didn't realize the effect the war would have on her state and family until she was thrust into it.

In letters to her sister in Ohio, Maggie describes how the women of Kansas faced the demons of the Civil War, fighting bravely to protect their homes and families while never knowing from one day to the next whether their men were alive or dead on a faraway battlefield.

I am writing this foreword on July 3, 1996. One hundred and fifty years ago today, Margaret Jane (Maggie) Kennedy Pieratt, my great-great grandmother, was born. I'm sure that her mother, Hannah Rumery Kennedy, never imagined at the moment of her birth that her daughter's life would illustrate one of the most important periods in America's history.

The Civil War caught Americans by surprise and forced them to cope with extraordinary circumstances. Maggie was just one of millions of women who had to live through this horrible situation.

Relive this war with a *Stitch of Courage*.

Leaving Home

January 24, 1861

"Do you remember Mamma?" Emma Pieratt's question catches me off guard. Which mother? Hers or mine?

It's an old game that the Pieratt girls and I used to play. Emma was very young, as I was when my mother, Hannah, left me. At least Sarah and George Ann were older when their mother, Deborah, died. The older sisters have tried to keep the memory going for Emma, but John remarried Nancy Shields that same year, and Emma thinks of her as their mother. But that's good—everyone needs a mother, or good memories of one.

I was fortunate to know Deborah Pieratt for a short time before she died. I was an orphaned sapling when I came to the territory in '58. Deborah died in '59 of consumption, a disease she couldn't defeat for her seven children, similar to the circumstances of my own mother.

My only memory of my mother is associated with quilts. Flashes of the scene still haunt me, although I was quite young at the time. I wasn't allowed past the doorway of a bedroom. I remember being held in someone's arms, probably one of my aunts, but this woman wouldn't let me down to run to my mother's side.

Why didn't my mother get up and take me into her arms, assuring me that everything would be all right?

I was looking in on a picture that I could not be a part of. My mother lay pale and wasted in the bed in the opposite corner of the room. Her body was lifeless except for her pleading eyes, longing to reach me, but apparently not daring to because of her contagious illness. She hadn't been ill long, but the disease had ravaged her body quickly, rendering it useless and malignant. Her eyes looked hollow, and her usually nice hair was a tangle coming out of its braid.

Although this was my last glimpse of my mother, I kept my eyes cast on the quilt that surrounded her, trying to avoid her gaze. I remember tracing the pattern on the quilt with my eyes, not wanting to look at her face. I imagined the patchwork of baskets and flowers coming alive so I could give them to my mother.

I would not answer her plea for a final good-bye. I turned my head away and hid my eyes in the crook of my aunt's neck. When she called my name, I looked to her for the last time through bleary eyes before I was taken from the doorway.

To this day, the bright colors of that Basket of Lilies quilt haunt me when I see red flowers—or smell death.

"It would have been her fortieth birthday today." Emma's remark pulls me from my thoughts.

Will I ever get over the feeling of abandonment?

Ever since I can remember, I've longed for my own home. I should have been young enough to adjust to another life, but the memories of the day of my mother's death still haunt me eleven years later. I don't think I'll feel secure until I have my own home, and children that I will promise never to leave behind.

January 29, 1861

Covering my ears for what seems the hundredth time, I brace myself for the latest firing of Old Sacramento. Mounted on top of Mount Oread, the cannon echoes throughout the territory. Smoke hangs in the frigid air, slowly dissipating over the area, mixing in with the constant pealing of the church bells. We have had two weeks of heavy snows, but townspeople and country folk alike now ignore the cold and surge the street corners, hugging, laughing, and crying for our good fortune. Hundreds crowd around the bonfires in the snow-covered town, braving the blistering January weather to celebrate the news.

Delivered to Leavenworth by telegraph from Washington, D.C., then by rider to Lawrence, the long-awaited news that Kansas has been admitted to statehood invited the neighborhood to commence a loud celebration at nine o'clock tonight.

The turmoil of the territory is over! Kansas has finally been added to the stars of the Union flag today after seven long years of difficulty and struggle. Our state may be the most poverty-stricken state ever to enter the Union, but we're here today to see it happen. Even if 30,000 people abandoned the state last year because of the drought, others stayed on because they knew the times would get better.

This is a major victory over slavery, the South, and Missouri. The ruins of the fort are visible on top of Mount Oread where the battles for righteousness were fought. They tried to make Kansas a proslavery state, but freedom was ultimately won!

But among the cheering tonight I have overheard groups talking about the discord in the South. While we have fought so hard to enter the Union, there are Southern states leaving it. Until I moved to Kansas and witnessed the territory's activities, I didn't understand the feelings and passions that stirred my Kennedy family to get involved in what I viewed as politics. Witnessing the situation and getting older, I realize they were drawn to their actions out of necessity.

When I arrived in the territory in 1858, most of the fighting was over between the proslavers and free-state people. It was the

Washington politicians that held up the final admittance to statehood.

My aunt, Margaret Kennedy, eight of her children, and their families and relatives traveled to the Kansas Territory in 1855. My brother, William James, trailed along, got work in a sawmill in Lawrence, and married fellow his traveler Lucinda Shields. Their moving to the new territory put them in the line of danger that threatened their lives and livelihood. Being strong Union patriots, they fought for the free-state issues and, luckily, survived the skirmishes.

I don't know if Aunt Phoebe Curless realized it or not, but while I was living with her I read every letter that Aunt Margaret sent to her from Kansas. Aunt Phoebe always tucked them in the back left corner of her top dresser drawer. Whenever the opportunity arrived that she would be gone for a spell, I would sneak out the letters, poring over my Aunt Margaret's words, reliving her accounts of her family's trip to the territory and the problems that followed. I felt that I knew every creek along the way and was prepared to venture into the territory myself. The territorial problems Aunt Margaret wrote about seemed unreal.

When William James traveled East to visit us, I begged him to take me to the territory with him because my closest sibling, John Alonzo, was going with him. My sister Mary Ann had remarried and had a houseful of two combined families. Brothers Moses and Michael had moved to Indiana. Sister Caroline had a wedding proposal, so I would lose her to marriage soon.

Ohio had always been my home, but I didn't feel connected to any certain house. Because my father's death preceded my mother's, I had to leave my childhood home and was shuffled among various relatives, whoever had room for me. Being the youngest of eleven children, I had siblings that were twenty-five years older than I, with families of their own. When one house got too crowded with new babies, I'd move to another. The only reason Aunt Phoebe let me go with my brothers was because she knew Aunt Margaret would look out for me at the other end.

William James became our legal guardian, and I was to move in with William James and Lucinda on their farm. The stark reality of the Plains stuck me as soon as I saw their log cabin. I got used to the wind blowing my skirts on the trail to Kansas, but I expected to reach civilization at the other end. As far as I was concerned, it wasn't in Kansas.

Instead of the paved roads and bridges we took for granted in Brown County, there were faint trails parting the tall prairie grass. Ohio's rolling landscape featured groves of huge trees with farms nestled in the clearings. Kansas was a continual stretch of grass, the only exception being the trees along the Wakarusa River.

The towns of Lawrence and Franklin, so often heard about, were nothing more than shantytowns compared to established Ohio.

There were no shortages of stores, because there were so many new businesses moving in, but boardwalks to keep a girl's skirt clean were absent. Schools were being held in whatever building was available, most often without blackboards, desks, or libraries.

I think the buildings I missed the most in the town's land-scape were churches. Right away I noticed there were no tall steeples pointing heavenward. It didn't seem right to sit in a building used for other purposes, instead of a church with the sunlight streaming through its stained glass windows. I didn't feel like God had found the Plains until I got used to it. The weather, be it sunshine, wind, rain, or snow—was brighter, stronger, heavier, harder—more severe even when it wasn't storming. When the clouds did reach their full turbulence, neither man, beast, nor vegetation could stand up to it.

The novelty and anticipation of life on the romantic Plains changed into the reality of rattlesnakes in tall grass, dirt floors in crude cabins, and never feeling quite clean. My former life as a merchant's daughter in the town of Hamersville, Ohio, changed forever when I left that state for the territory of Kansas.

I packed bonnets, but they were impractical and silly-looking compared to the other girls' headgear. I wore everyday dresses on the trail but was expecting to don my fine-tailored clothes after my arrival. I found out shoes and stockings were only worn for church or cold weather in Kansas. Most children went barefoot from the first warm thaw to the last fall frost.

Social events weren't numerous at first because people were putting all their time and energy into building new farms out on the prairie. I was needed to tend the garden instead of spending hours perfecting my stitchery skills with a circle of friends.

Of course, homesickness for Ohio and my two older sisters, Mary Ann and Caroline, set in after my arrival. I was embarrassed to let on to my Aunt Phoebe how much I missed our cultured life in Ohio, or how primitive I thought our Kansas relatives had become. So in my letters to Caroline I vented my feelings, good and bad, as I adjusted to the simple life on the Plains, and to my growth from child to young woman.

Over time I grew to know the settlers in our neighborhood, and they became an extension of my family. The people who live here are a variety of former citizens from other states. Groups, families, and solitary people rushed into the territory when it was opened. This mixture has created problems but also a rich stew.

My first friends, the Pieratt children, were from Kentucky originally. Besides farming, the Pieratts run a store in Franklin. Robert is my age, Belvard and James are older than I and their three sisters—Sarah, George Ann, and Emma—are younger. John Franklin brought up the end of the family until their mother died and their father remarried.

John Pieratt's second wife, Nancy, is my sister-in-law, Lucinda's sister. Because of these sisters our families are together quite often, whether it be to combine forces on tasks or just to visit.

I also spend time in the Kennedy Valley. Aunt Margaret and her family have built a stronghold of farms running through the rich valley of the Wakarusa River. They have expanded not only in acres but in members, so I'm over often to help with the babies.

Yes, the start of my life on the plains was a rough change, but my young spirit helped me adjust to the Kansas prairie.

"Come on," a school friend urges. "Let's go join in the singing over by that bonfire!" A robust version of a patriotic song catches on and ascends with the smoke that filters into the sky. As we crowd into the warmth of the circle, I see my reflection in the flames. I wonder what this new year and the changes it brings for the Union will mean for the fourteen-year-old I see dancing in the light.

A Union Star

Thursday, February 28, 1861
Franklin, Kansas

Dear Caroline,

Greetings from the new state of Kansas! I can't say I see much change, but the grownups think it will make a world of difference to be a part of the Union.

Abraham Lincoln raised the first flag with Kansas's thirty-fourth star over Independence Hall in Philadelphia last week on his way to Washington, D.C., for his inauguration. People here say it is a good sign that we'll have a better year.

Weather has turned to spring after last month's horrible conditions. With the moisture we have been receiving, farmers are anxious to plant and forget last year's drought. They are watching for the steamer from Atchinson that is to deliver the seed.

Everyone at school has been pining to be outdoors instead of inside the store where we hold our sessions. The boys are ready to quit studying and start the spring field work. Some of their antics have tried the patience of our teacher. He's ready to put them behind a team of plow horses for sure!

Distractions seem to be normal these days. Talk of the problems between the states is heard in the store and the streets. It seems to drift into our classroom and our studies. Our map of the states is examined often, especially after we read the newspaper reports.

I doubt I will go back to school when it commences next winter. I'll be fifteen by then, and I've had more schooling than most of the students anyway. I know my numbers, prose and poetry, so it is time to move out of the classroom. In some ways I will miss it, but I'll be needed at home with Lucinda having another baby this summer. She has her hands full with Alonzo and Mary the way it is.

Between schoolwork and family duties, I've been edging my latest quilt top, the Rocky-Road-to-Kansas. When this one is done I'll have seven finished quilts. Lucinda thinks I should have a dozen made for my hope chest.

Do you have any new patterns you could send me? Aunt Margaret has lots of old patterns, but I'd like some new ones.

The Pieratt girls and Nancy were over last Saturday to quilt. Emma took care of the young children, so we had five of us around the frame. With so many new children in the growing Kennedy families, it seems like we are quilting somewhere every Saturday. Every house has a basket of sewing projects sitting by the rocker to be worked on in spare time.

You asked about our brother, John Alonzo. His last letter to Kansas said he may be heading back here soon. He spent last fall mining along the Blue River on Kansas's western border (or I should say in the new Colorado Territory, because our state border has been changed), then was a clerk in a store for the winter. His letters have been few and far between, because it costs twenty-five cents to go between here and Denver, but it only takes six days by stagecoach. It has been exciting to hear about the mountains and the growth of the area. The news of the secession of seven Southern states traveled along with the freight to Denver.

I don't know what the Confederate States of America or their new president, Jefferson Davis, plan to do, but it has been the talk of the area since Southern troops seized nearly all the federal forts within the South.

William James says this secession talk is affecting our money. Bills from Illinois that were largely founded on the stock of Southern states are not being accepted in banks or stores. Kansas doesn't have its own currency, so what will we do if the money from other states fails? The adults tell me not to worry about it, but politics are discussed at every meal. There is no way *not* to know what is going on when you live among the Kennedys!

I enjoyed the poetry you included in your last letter, so I have included a poem from our *Kansas State Journal*. It seems to fit the times, so I thought I would pass it on.

I look forward to your next letter. Please write what the Kennedys and Curlesses are up too. I still miss our cousins at times.

Patriotically adding a star,

Maggie

Saturday, May 11 , 1861
Franklin, Kansas

Dear Caroline,

Thought I would write to occupy my mind. While cleaning today I came across a little ball of Alonzo's. It must have rolled under the bed sometime and was never retrieved until now.

Even though it has been two months since our nephew's death, I still think of him every day. I catch myself daydreaming of his chubby checks flushed with excitement at the silliest of games, or framed with his dark lashes in his slumber. Children are so precious.

The house is quiet without his rambunctious behavior. He'd try to act like a perfect angel while saying his bedtime prayer, although he may have terrorized the household a few hours before.

Poor baby Mary is being smothered between Lucinda's and my constant attention. Mary keeps looking for Alonzo every place she can toddle to.

I know he was Lucinda's child, but I helped raise him since birth and I still cry thinking about seeing him slip away. Even though death seems to haunt the prairie, I wasn't prepared to lose someone so dear to me. I hope I never have to lose a child of my own someday.

Everything seems so unsettled and unsure right now. Our newspaper had a big headline stating "War Commenced! Bombardment of Ft. Sumter" after South Carolina attacked the fort in Charleston Harbor. We were shocked when the U.S. flag was lowered. I guess we all thought that the problems between the Union and Confederates could be solved peacefully, without military force.

Did any of your neighbors enlist when Lincoln called up men for the militia last month? 75,000 men seems like a lot to me. Although Kansas was not assigned a quota because we are so far away from the situation, several hundred men signed up to join the Northern army and crush the rebellion. Everyone agrees the revolt must be checked and the Union flag put back up over all the eleven states that have left it.

Our new senator, James Lane, who is now in Washington, D.C., for the session, formed a group of Kansas men to guard the White House since the siege. With the capitol being right on the edge of the Confederate states, it is assumed that they will attack that town next.

Everyone is wondering how this war will affect the uneasy situation between Kansas and Missouri. Supposedly this war is about the states leaving the Union, but many people feel the underlying problem is the slave issue. Most Kansans do not welcome blacks into the state because they do not want them living in our communities. But Kansas become antislavery because of Missouri trying to force it to become a proslavery state. Many people here have friends and relatives in Missouri, but they remember the border ruffians and how they tried to control the land and government.

There was talk after church today that if Missouri joins the Confederacy, Kansas would be cut off from the rest of the nation. I think that is why more men did not join Lincoln's call. They feel they must stay here and guard our own border.

You know all the problems that "Bleeding Kansas" had with the border wars. We're all hoping history does not repeat itself—and I pray I'll not get caught in the middle of it.

Early yesterday morning Aunt Margaret came by our house in the big lumber wagon with a load of feed sacks piled high. She asked Lucinda if it was all right that I ride along with her. At the time I didn't realize it but Lucinda did not say yes until Aunt Margaret emphasized that she needed to conduct business up north. I thought it was odd that one of her sons or grandsons were not with her, but I was glad to get out of the day's planned chores.

We had gone only two miles when someone sneezed right behind me! I nearly jumped off the wagon seat. Aunt Margaret kept staring ahead, talking like she didn't hear a thing. The sound was loud enough that you couldn't help but hear it. When I started to ask her about the noise, she just shook her head and put a finger to her lips to silence me.

It dawned on me then that we were transporting some runaway slaves that were hidden underneath the sacks of grain. I had never helped before, that I know of. I thought runaways were usually transported at night, but here she and I were doing it during broad daylight!

I was petrified every time we passed someone on the road after that. There are men patrolling the area all the time looking for runaways and the people who help them. There are rewards out for both and we could have ended up in jail, or worse.

I couldn't believe that Lucinda would let me go if she knew what Aunt Margaret was doing. But then, being a Quaker family, Lucinda's parents may be helping out also. That is one of the strange things about the Underground Railroad. There must be hundreds of people helping the slaves escape to Canada, but you don't know who the conductors are because it is all done in secret.

One trio of gruff horsemen stopped in our path near our destination. I thought I would faint from fright, but Aunt Margaret said under her breath, "Hold your Kennedy head high, Margaret Jane, and don't say a word." When she uses my given name, I know she means business. The men asked questions, poked the sacks with their rifles, and then let the "old lady" and her niece pass. I did not breathe for five whole minutes.

We pulled to a stop in front of the Hiatt House. Aunt Margaret asked the manager to take the wagon into the barn to feed and water the horses. This didn't seem unusual because it is a way station, except for how she worded it. Usually you unhitch the team instead of driving the wagon inside the barn. We retired to the house for refreshments, then got back into the wagon when it appeared out front again. Apparently the cargo was unloaded and hidden someplace safe until they could move on to the next leg of their journey.

Aunt Margaret wouldn't answer most of my questions on our journey back home. She said the less I knew, the better off I was if I was ever questioned. I'm not even sure she knew herself how many Negroes were hidden in the wagon.

I imagine Doc Jennison and his Jayhawkers raided Missouri in the past few days, liberated some slaves, and needed help moving them up the line. I know Cousin Bridge has gone to visit the Hiatts twice this month, so apparently he has been helping the cause also. I'm expected to keep my mouth sealed to protect the runaways and the people who help them, so you are the only person I mentioned this trip to.

When we got back to the house, the family was sitting down to supper. Lucinda asked if my "day of quilting over at Aunt Margaret's" was successful. Not a word was said about my ride. I don't think William James even knew where I went. Apparently the Kennedy women have a few causes of their own that not all Kennedy men know about.

Please say a prayer to keep your little sister safe.

Helping the cause,

Maggie

Wednesday, July 31, 1861
Franklin, Kansas

Dear Caroline,

I'm going to take advantage of the few quiet minutes I have to write while the children are taking a nap. Nancy Pieratt gave birth to a little girl this morning, so Lucinda is helping her sister, and I have the little ones here. Lucinda is about to deliver any day now, too. If all goes well, we'll have two babies in the house again.

It has been a hot day in which to keep the children happy and occupied. I spread a blanket on the shady side of the house to escape the heat inside. We made a picnic out of our dinner, and that seemed to soothe their tummies and tempers.

Lately I've been as restless as the dust devils. I wish I was on my own like our brothers. I thought about traveling back to Ohio. William James says I'm being a bother thinking such things, but Lucinda seems to understand my feelings. Both said I cannot travel back to Ohio because of the war threat.

I've never thought of it before, because I've always had a home, but I have always been an extra person in someone else's family. Although I'm afraid of the miseries of pregnancy, I want children of my own someday. Am I wrong in longing for a home and family of my own? Did you feel that way when you were growing up? Since we were separated so much of the time, I don't know if you felt this way, too.

No, I can not report I have a beau yet. All the boys are infatuated with the war news and not paying attention to the girls in their midst. I'm afraid I'll have my trousseau done and its contents will yellow with age before I'm engaged.

Several of us went fishing last weekend, but all I caught was my dress sleeve on a plum thorn and a sunburn.

We did have a good turnout at the Fourth of July celebration in town. (Did Aunt Margaret write that she had another grandchild born on Independence Day? That is the second time it has happened on the Fourth. That was Tom and Martha's baby. Leander and Amanda's will come next month.) Most of the

16

Kennedys went into town for the celebration, which consisted of speeches of a patriotic nature. We can't escape its mention these days. Now there is always a column in our weekly paper with war news—reports from different states, war vessels blockading the Atlantic coast and down to the Gulf of Mexico, groups practicing their marching, and on and on.

Senator Lane is back in the state, saying men are to "rally to the stars & stripes, and come forward." He wants to get three regiments enlisted and trained. There is a new Fort Lincoln being built on the Little Osage River, north of Fort Scott, to have troops close to the border in case of a raid.

Governor Robinson called the citizens to form a militia in mid June because there were Union and Confederate groups fighting in Jefferson City, Missouri. Men lined the Kansas border but nothing crossed the state line except for rebel Missourians. Hundreds of western Missouri Unionists have fled into Kansas for protection. Many men have joined Kansas troops and are raiding Missouri to retrieve their things. William James and our cousins have gone to several home guard meetings to talk about protecting our homes in case of an invasion. Every one is worked up over this threat.

Aunt Margaret seems to be preparing for battle—hiding valuables, stocking up the cellar, hoarding bullets. She says she must be prepared if they get raided, as they did during the early years of the territory.

John Pieratt, Nancy's husband, has taken the stand that he and his sons will not take part in the war because of their ties with the border state of Kentucky. His oldest son, Belvard, just became a minister and does not want to have anything to do with killing. On the other hand, John's younger sons, James Monroe and Robert, are itching to see some fighting.

There was some vague news sent by telegraph about a fight at Bull Run, a stream near Manassas, Virginia, ten days ago. Supposedly the Confederate side won, so the North is trying to put more troops together to take care of the war. Because little action has taken place, I think both sides are getting tired of the news. We thought the war would be over in three months.

People are uneasy that the Confederates have moved their capitol from Alabama to Richmond, Virginia. It being, along with Washington, D.C., on the East Coast, makes all this war talk seem so far way. Even though four more states joined the Confederacy, Missouri decided to stay with the Union, so most people here feel safe about that.

I think our current worry is that the Cherokees are stirring up troubles in southeast Kansas. We're liable to have an attack from either the Indian Territory or Confederate Arkansas before we have problems with soldiers from Richmond, Virginia, raiding us.

In the meantime we are harvesting a bumper crop this summer. Last year's drought emptied the bins, but this year's spring rains are filling them up again. As the men travel around to the different homesteads to harvest, I've been going with them to help prepare the meals. I'm sick of making a dozen pies every morning. I'll be glad when the wheat and oats are threshed.

The new Pieratt birth meant someone else had to make my share of pastries today. Don't worry, I'll be sure to thank them for their toil.

I will write when we have another nephew or niece in the family.

Restless with the rest of Kansas,

Maggie

Friday, September 10, 1861
Franklin, Kansas

Dear Caroline,

We committed a second child to the ground. Mary Caroline died Saturday. I know that nature takes its course with every living being, but it is so hard to accept when it is a little child you've grown to love.

Losing two children in less than a year is almost more than William James and Lucinda can bear. Our brother goes around doing his daily chores in a trance. Lucinda's sisters or her mother have taken turns being here since she gave birth to the new baby last month, then stayed on to help when Mary Caroline grew ill. Lucinda has stayed in bed most of the time, weak from childbirth and misery.

I think right now she is afraid to love little Lizzie Jane for fear she will grow attached to another child who might have the same fate as the first two. Lucinda is nursing her but doesn't want to hold her otherwise.

I'm helping out the best I can with the cooking and laundry but lament that I can do nothing to heal Lucinda's suffering. I'm afraid that is something that we must all bear with in our own way.

Aunt Margaret said that since the new baby's middle name is the same as mine, (and hers) Lizzie and I will always have a special bond like she and I have had. She said I should take Lizzie under my wing and give her special guidance. I think Aunt Margaret was trying to help me overcome my fears.

The poor little thing does look a little like me. I pray that she has a longer future than her siblings and that I can help her grow into a healthy, happy child.

Please give a tight hug to your children for me. I'm afraid morbid fear has me worrying about all my nephews and nieces.

Crushed with worry and loss,

Maggie

Thursday, October 11, 1861
Franklin, Kansas

Dear Caroline,

Things seem to be getting worse around here instead of better. How has the war affected the Kennedy and Curless families in Ohio? I worry about Phoebe's boys. I haven't heard from that branch of the family for quite some time.

Problems with the Confederate Army in Missouri are keeping our state on alert. There are small groups of Union soldiers going in and out of the area on a regular basis now. It is not uncommon to see them going down the California Road that runs through Franklin on their way to and from the border and Lawrence.

General Price and his Confederate troops from southwest Missouri and Arkansas defeated and killed General Lyon in August at the battle of Wilson's Creek near Springfield, Missouri. Senator Lane's Kansas Brigade has been sweeping through Missouri, trying to clear the valley of bushwhackers and Confederates. They cleaned out Osceola in late September, so Price couldn't use the town for his winter headquarters. Lane freed slaves from Rebel masters and confiscated Rebel property for the use of the federal government.

This raid was said to be in retaliation for the Missourians' raid on Humbolt, Kansas, last month. People have mixed feelings about Lane's actions. They fear that his maneuvers into Missouri will cause bitter hatred toward Kansas. Hearing that Lane's Brigade was in western Missouri, the Confederates then attacked the group during the first part of September near Drywood Creek, Missouri. When Lane retreated back to Kansas, it was feared that Price would follow and attack Fort Scott, but that did not happen.

According to yesterday's newspaper, the Union surrendered at Lexington, Missouri, to Price on September 20 after 3,600 Union men held off 18,000 Confederate soldiers for nine days. The Confederates captured the Union troops only because they advanced behind wet bales of hemp.

There have been signs openly posted around town for the men to join the commissioned Jennison and Independent Mounted Kansas Jayhawkers. John Brown, Jr. is in the group. Cousin Tom has been riding with Lane, also.

General John C. Frémont, in charge of the Military Department of the West, wanted to invoke martial law, confiscate the property of all Missourians who had taken up arms against the Union, and free their slaves, but President Lincoln forbade carrying out this idea. Lincoln does not want to lose the loyalty of the four slave states that stayed in the Union when the war began, of which Missouri is one. These states form a barrier between the two factions.

Goodness, all I've done is repeat the news of the war and our problems here to you. I hope you aren't having the same problems in Ohio. I can't imagine Kentuckians or other state citizens raiding across the border the way the Missourians do here.

It has also been posted that the Douglas County Agricultural and Mechanical Society will postpone their annual exhibit for one year because of the war.

So many things that we young people enjoy have been postponed and canceled this fall because of the war. I know the cause of the war is justified, but it seems like such a waste of life and energy. I hope things will be settled by Christmas so it does not spoil our holiday season.

Please continue to write so I know that all of the family is safe in Ohio.

Watching the border,

Maggie

Uneasy Borders

Saturday, March 15, 1862
Franklin, Kansas

Dear Caroline,

Thank you for the valentine. I hope you received mine also. I bought my cards from Pieratt's store and sent several but received cards only from you and the Pieratt family. Of course they didn't have to pay for them, since the cards were from their father's store, so they passed them out freely to friends.

Harper's Weekly had advertised a soldier's valentine packet containing six valentines and envelopes for fifty-one cents. I wonder if the advertisers thought the soldiers would have six sweethearts at home, or did they expect them to divide the cards up among their fellow soldiers?

I make this comment because we have subscribed to *Harper's Weekly* now. It has good illustrated coverage of the war so we can keep informed. Most evenings William James reads out loud while Lucinda and I do our handiwork, so I know everything that is going on in the nation.

Do you get news of the fighting going on in the Plains and west of us? The battles going on in the mountains of the West have been the latest news. Troops from Denver are on their way to the New Mexico Territory because the Confederates have taken Albuquerque and Santa Fe and are now attacking Fort Union.

The Confederates are trying to annex a corridor from the Rio Grande in Texas all the way to the Pacific Coast of California. They hope the Spanish and the Mormons will help the Southern cause. The Indians are indirectly helping because the federal troops are out chasing them due to their disruptions along the trade routes. The mineral wealth of the West could finance the war and extend slavery into five new territories and states. William James said that if the Confederacy claims the Colorado Territory, we'd have trouble on three sides of Kansas.

I assume you read that President Lincoln's son Willie died? The poor man has enough to worry about with the nation amongst itself, and then this happens. I truly feel for him and his wife.

We had callers today. The older man was an acquaintance of our brother and, I assumed, came over to talk business. His son, a homely sort with greasy hair, was also along. It wasn't long before I realized they had come over for this young man to meet me!

William James and the man excused themselves to look at stock, leaving me to entertain the boy. Lucinda stayed in the kitchen just far enough to hear what was going on but not close enough to help out with the conversation.

The only thing he wanted to talk about was the war situation, nothing on social events, books, or music. Spring weather and planting got us through another five minutes and then we sat in silence for what seemed like hours.

I rose in relief from my enforced hospitality when the men returned, only to hear William James invite them to stay for dinner! I escaped to help Lucinda prepare the meal, but the oaf followed me into the kitchen and watched me peel potatoes.

They lingered another hour after the meal. William James tried to suppress his smile until after he ushered them out the door. Then he had the nerve to tease me about having a new beau. Our brother got a dish rag thrown in his face for that remark.

What can I do about unwanted callers?

Surrounded by conflicts,

Maggie

Saturday, May 3, 1862
Franklin, Kansas

Dear Caroline,

Greetings from your Kansas Kennedy clan. I have not written for a while, so I thought I'd take time this morning and mail the letter posthaste.

Yesterday we were in Lawrence for errands. I had not been there for quite some time and was surprised by all the activity going on. The hotels, boardinghouses, and boardwalks were crowded with soldiers. I suppose they are congregating from other parts of the state to organize their regiments. Few of them have uniforms on, but they usually have some sort of homespun blue shirt that a wife or mother made.

So many young men in town, and none of them interested in me. Maybe it is best that I don't have someone to worry about in this war.

Gossip was buzzing so fast in the stores that it was difficult to concentrate on our shopping. Of course it was sometimes hard to distinguish fact from brag, but it was certainly colorful and exciting. The Union's victory at Shiloh, Tennessee, last month is still the talk of the town.

We were relieved to hear that the Union Navy has captured New Orleans. We needed to cut off that port because the Confederates were moving their supplies to their troops up the Mississippi River. They were also exporting their produce to Europe through that port to pay for their import needs.

Lincoln's main strategy is to cut off the South from the world's supplies. It is a slow method, but by depriving them of food and supplies we will eventually exhaust the South. Union troops are instructed to burn the South's crops, factories, homes, railroads, and bridges as they pass through. The newspaper is calling Lincoln's approach the Conda, after the Anaconda, a huge snake that kills its prey by squeezing.

Actually, Kansas is profiting from the war. Our crops and livestock are being sold to the Union Army. Last year's bumper crop might be duplicated this year if we go by the favorable weather we're having. We can sell as many horses, mules, and cattle as we can raise in the county. We might not have many men in the actual battles, but we're certainly doing our share to help the war effort.

Of course, problems exist here. Raids from bushwhackers still continue along the border. A William Quantrill and his gang raided Aubry in Johnson County this spring. Someone thought that this same man, called Charlie Hart then, was prosecuted in Lawrence two years ago for burglary, arson, kidnapping, and horse stealing. I think Dr. Williams, John Pieratt's store partner, was a juror on that trial. Hart disappeared before starting his sentence.

There are also Indian refugees camped from here down to the Neohso Valley around Leroy, Kansas. Indians are coming up from the Indian Territory because the agents are not providing them with food and clothing, as the government promised they would. No wonder they are attacking settlers around the country.

While in town I bought material for a summer dress. I want something new to catch the right man's eye at the picnics and gatherings that usually go on in the summer. I also bought a new hoop for my skirts. My old one had worn out and I had been using a loop of grapevine to give my skirt the flare it needed. Of course it was lopsided, but it worked in a pinch. I wore my old crinoline while shopping in town, but the stiff petticoat is too hot for me in the summer. Besides, I want to wear what's in fashion.

What are women wearing in Ohio these days? I'll look forward to your answer. I don't want to be seen in anything but the proper dress of the North.

Gossiping in town,

Maggie

Friday, August 8, 1862
Franklin, Kansas

Dear Caroline,

I've been watching a glorious sunset while I write to you. Our evenings are usually spent outside on the porch to escape the heat of the house. We don't reenter the house until it's time to retire. Some nights I've even returned to the porch floor to sleep if it's too stifling inside.

Cousin Bridge, Elizabeth, and their four children sit with us this mellow evening. Earlier in the day we women and children hunted patches of elderberries, then the men joined us for an evening picnic.

Bridge said that the Union volunteers have slowed to a trickle because people are tired of the nightmare that war had brought upon the nation. Fights for the past two months around the Shenandoah Valley, Virginia, are worrying people because the Union did not take Richmond as planned.

Senator Lane received a War Department commission this summer to raise troops for the army. The new General Lane is telling people that unless there are enough Kansans who enlist voluntarily, there will be a draft to raise the count needed. Cousin Tom Kennedy has already signed up as a recruiting officer and raised one hundred men in nine days. His Company B, in the 12th Kansas Volunteers, is ordered to report to Fort Lincoln this fall for a three-year stint. I hope we are not wrong in assuming it will never last that long.

Tom's wife, Martha, has resigned herself to the fact that he feels he must do his duty. At least being in the Kennedy Valley she'll have help with their farm and family.

Lucinda's brother, William Shields, and Robert Pieratt both signed up to go with Tom. I couldn't believe Mr. Pieratt let Robert sign up. He is too young, only sixteen, like me.

General Lane has placed advertisements in newspapers state-wide urging white and black men to join his ranks. Because Kansas has a small Negro population, he is encouraging slaves from Missouri to escape across the border to join up. Lane is offering the runaways a certificate of freedom, but less pay than that of a white soldier. I would think that these men would worry about their families being left behind if they fled their Missouri masters.

Free Negro men in other states have tried to enlist but have been told no, it is a white man's war. People are uneasy here to think of fighting side by side with a Negro, but most also agree that they could become targets for Rebel gunpowder just as much as a white man.

Negroes are starting to see this war as a fight for the freedom of their people. Some light-skinned men have enlisted by pretending to be white. Others I hear are helping out as cooks and laborers. Free women are working as laundresses, seamstresses, and nurses to the troops. Many have no home, so they are trailing along, helping out to be allowed to stay and keep their menfolk in sight.

Many people are ignoring the Union's plight and are heading to the western part of Kansas to stake a claim. When Lincoln's Homestead Act took effect the last part of May, families streamed through here to take advantage of the free acres being offered on public land. All the homesteaders have to do is build a home and stay and farm it for five years, and the deed becomes theirs. The President hopes the rapid settlement of the West will strengthen the Union. We'll see what happens.

I hope you are enjoying a pleasant evening, too.

Watching the changing population,

Maggie

Wednesday, September 24, 1862
Franklin, Kansas

Dear Caroline,

I'm a little blue, so I thought I would write to my dear sister.

Yesterday we said good-bye to several family members in the 12th Kansas Infantry that left for Paola. Cousin Tom was elected Major of the group. Of course we were proud of him, and of the others who enlisted, but I worry that we won't see them again.

I didn't realize how attached I had become to Robert Pieratt until he enlisted. I'm still not sure if he feels the same or just considers me his family's friend.

Last Sunday we sat outside on the wagon talking until William James came out to say it was time for me to come in and for Robert to go home. Robert tenderly held my hand as we gazed at the stars. It was probably just a gesture to assure me he'll be all right away from home, but it set my heart to flutter. I gave him one of my blue hair ribbons to remember me by while he's gone. I plan to write to him regularly and sincerely wish he will do the same. It puts a new perspective on what I read about the war, because now I'll picture Robert as the soldier who is facing the battle.

What if he has to fight in a battle like the one on Antietam Creek near Sharpsburg, Maryland, last week? The newspaper said it was the bloodiest day of the war so far, and neither side could claim a victory. At least General Lee's advance has been stopped and he had to turn his troops back to Virginia.

One of Robert's regiment assignments will probably be stopping the guerrilla raiding. The first part of the month Quantrill raided Olathe. The 10th Kansas Regiment pursued and recovered most of the loot in Pleasant Hill, Missouri, on the 19th. They burned homes of that neighborhood to destroy the guerrilla headquarters and brought back sixty slaves with them.

Lincoln announced this week that if the states of rebellion did not return to the Union by January 1 of next year, he would declare their slaves forever free. Do you think that the Southern states would actually let their property go? I hope the states decide to rejoin the Union so Robert can come home.

I'm keeping occupied by the amount of work this year's harvest has produced. The late garden is being picked and preserved now. Each day another section of the garden is cleared of its produce. We added the last of the cucumbers to the brine Monday after the weekly washing. Tuesday we pickled another batch of beets. Today's project has been pitting and halving late plums to dry. Pumpkins, turnips, and drying beans will be left a few more weeks.

We've picked up a wagonload of watermelons the first of the week, sending most of that haul with the troops. William James donated a wagonful of produce, from potatoes to flour, to send along with Tom. It was a way to help, because he is staying here in Kansas on the farm.

Farmers have been working night and day to supply the Union with food. What isn't used on the western posts are sent east by freight wagons. Unfortunately, there is always the chance that the Confederates or Missouri Rebels will confiscate it. But as Lucinda put it, it will still be getting into a soul who needs nourishment.

It won't be long before frost covers the last of the vines and the garden is plowed under to rest until spring. There is already a slight hint of yellow tinge showing on the trees around here. The air is more crisp in the morning, and the sunset is arriving sooner. The songbirds will soon be leaving as the branches turn bare on the trees.

And we're going into another season of war.

Saying good-bye to summer and our boys,

Maggie

Friday, November 7, 1862
Franklin, Kansas

Dear Caroline,

Cousin Zanetta said they received a letter from her husband's family in Illinois. Two of Will's brothers, Lafayette and Edmond Curless, signed up for three-year stints in Peoria in August. They thought they were leaving trouble behind when they left Bleeding Kansas, but this war has affected every state of the Union.

The bushwhackers are why most of our men did not answer General Lane's call this fall. They need to stay here with arms ready for invaders. Lane did round up enough men, though, for the 11th, 12th, and 13th Regiments and the 1st and 2nd Kansas Colored Volunteers.

In last week's election the state voted Republican through the whole ticket. Thomas Carney is our new governor now, so we'll see if that changes our involvement in the war.

Quantrill is in the news again. He sacked and burned Shawneetown a few weeks ago. He is threatening to give Lawrence a call. Late last Sunday night the word of danger raced through the neighborhood. William James and every other able man in the vicinity was assembled in town an hour later. We have all been through the raids and know how serious they can be.

We readied our home defense by keeping a pot of water boiling over the fire with dipper handy to throw scalding pain on our attackers. There was a club behind the door and an ax hanging over it where William James had taken the gun off its rack. Luckily, our defense skills were not tested.

Currently our troops are in Arkansas chasing the Confederates back over the Arkansas River. We heard that the 12th Regiment participated in the battle at Prairie Grove, Arkansas, last month, which prevented the Confederates from coming into the West. We have not heard any news about the family members involved.

How is your currency situation in Ohio? I've read that in some places money is so scarce that stamps are being used as currency. Our postmaster in Franklin says there is a new government law that any stamp bought must be glued on the letter in front of him and mailed immediately. You've probably heard the saying lately that "many a one parting with a silver dollar would squeeze it so hard the eagle would holler." At least we're not to the point of melting down church bells to be cast into guns and shells, as the South is doing.

I wish I could hear from Robert again. I've sent three letters but have received only one reply. The postmaster assured me that letters were getting to and from the troops. He suggested that Robert didn't have the time right now because he might be on the move chasing Rebels.

Mr. Pieratt said they had not heard at all, so I shared Robert's letter with his family. There were two lines at the bottom of the page I did not read out loud because they were meant to be private between us, but I was glad to ease their minds about their son. Since he talked mainly about food, Nancy worried that he must be hungry and vowed to take care of that immediately.

Robert said they called the hardtack "worm castles" because sometimes it was so old that they would find live worms when biting into the biscuit. He added what I hope was a joke about these crackers. "Breaking open hardtack and finding worms in it, a soldier threw the spoiled crackers in a trench. Later, an officer got mad at this soldier because he had told him to clean out the trench for sanitary reasons, and the crackers were still there. The soldier explained, 'Sir, we've thrown it out two or three times, but it keeps crawling back!'"

I assume you will be baking and sending Oliver some of your best soda biscuits and gingersnaps in the near future after reading this joke. We're sending several boxes to Company B in the 12th Kansas Volunteers.

Baking for our soldiers,

Maggie

Saturday, December 27, 1862
Franklin, Kansas

Dear Caroline,

I pray you had a peaceful holiday season. Was Oliver able to be with you and the children for Christmas? Think of all the families that were separated from their menfolk, temporarily or permanently, this month because of this war.

Fortunately I was able to see Robert, because his company was camped at the Lawrence fairgrounds until yesterday. I think our cousin Major Kennedy arranged it so his volunteers could be close to their families for Christmas Day. Tom also wanted to see his new daughter, Martha Belle. William and Robert were able to leave camp Christmas afternoon for a family meal. We joined the Pieratts, Shields, and our family together so Nancy and Lucinda could see their brothers.

The table was loaded with everything the men had been craving while out in the field, and then some. The aroma of the ham, turkey, preserves, and fresh-baked bread lasted longer in the house than the actual food. Robert said it sure beats the "What-have-you" stew they usually have to dine on.

We restocked their supplies before they marched for Arkansas. The government is supposed to feed our troops, but the sparse rations lack variety and substance. Every woman in the area baked extra bread and pies to feed the troops. Cellars were unloaded of candles, meat, dried fruit—anything to stock the company supply wagon. Old clothing was stripped and rolled into bandages for battle wounds. Several men gave the coats off their backs to young soldiers who did not have adequate warmth.

I gave Robert my latest quilt as a Christmas present. I know the Wild Goose Chase is doomed to become a muddy rag before the end of winter, but it was going to a good cause. Robert had it rolled up and wrapped around his shoulder when I saw him marching out of town. They were singing Christmas carols and the new song, "The Battle Hymn of the Republic." I'll sing Glory, Glory, Hallelujah when this war is over. With the Union defeats at Fredericksburg, Virginia, and Murfreesboro, Tennessee, this month, there is no telling how far this Kansas regiment may be walking this year.

I had a few hours with Robert before he left. He was in a holiday mood, but much more reserved and quiet than when he left in September. Robert didn't say much about the battles in Arkansas, but I could tell that what he saw and experienced changed his thoughts on the adventures and glory of war.

When the war is over, what kind of a man will he be—ready to forget the past and tackle the future—or stuck in the war, reliving the battles he lived through? Robert is so young. I wonder how this war will affect the rest of his life.

Of course, I'm beginning to wonder the same about me.

Wishing you a healthy new year,

Maggie

Raids of Destruction

Friday, January 16, 1863
Franklin, Kansas

Dear Caroline,

It's a cold, dreary day, with hints of flurries every so often. I can't recall the sun showing its rays this week. I need to go to the store this afternoon, so I thought I'd pen you a letter before I bundle up and brave the elements.

My project this month has been knitting socks for our soldiers, and I need more yarn. Any spare time is being spent for the cause. All us Kennedy women plan to combine our handiwork and send it to Cousin Tom's troop next week. We've made over two dozen socks, a large bundle of rolled bandages, and six small quilts. Actually, we cut up three old quilts and patched and reinforced the edges to make pallet-sized ones.

Lucinda donated her grandmother's Irish Puzzle, a huge old quilt that made its way over many miles before being patched for its next voyage. I think it possibly came from Ireland when her mother, Mary, left that country. We're seeing the same pattern being called the Kansas Troubles now.

Remember Cousin Nettie's Stepping Stones? You might have helped quilt that one because it was made before she was married.

The third quilt was Aunt Margaret's Eternal Triangle. I bit my lip to stop my tears when she cut it apart, because it had always been a favorite of mine. I remember it being on her bed downstairs. I couldn't imagine her cutting up a quilt that she had shared with her husband. Apparently she thought it was beyond repair and memories and could be of more use in the field to some cold soul than to her linen chest.

The whole community has contributed as much clothing, blankets, and food as they can spare. It is the least we can do for the men while they are braving the war alone.

It has been a horribly cold winter so far. I have on extra layers under my skirt today and I'm still cold. But I think of the men sleeping in canvas tents out in this weather, and then I am truly thankful I have a roof over my head and a warm hearth at my feet.

The neighborhood children haven't been complaining, though. The abundance of snow has made superb sledding conditions. I even took a few runs yesterday afternoon. The children have time because they are out of school for two weeks to keep the smallpox from spreading. It was best to cancel school to cut the epidemic. The sick ones are at home recuperating and the healthy ones are enjoying the break.

The cold winter has postponed confrontations and put most of the soldiers in winter quarters here. I hate to think what bloodshed this spring will bring.

We are bound to see some changes with President Lincoln signing the Emancipation Proclamation. Declaring that all slaves living in the states fighting against the Union are now free is a daring move. Lincoln believes that freeing the slaves is the best way to undermine the Confederacy and assure a Union victory. Losing the slaves will cripple the South and force the white men into working the fields instead of fighting the Union Army. Mr. Pieratt said it did not affect the slaves in the loyal border states, though. That means that the Negroes in Missouri are still slaves.

We're seeing more Negroes enlisting in the army now that they are allowed to. I read that in South Carolina they had a program to give a colored regiment a Union flag. Someone started signing "My country, 'tis of thee, sweet land of liberty." Just think of it! The first day they have ever had a country and a flag that promised anything to their people. The black men in Union uniform around here seem to stand taller and prouder. One commented that it was the biggest thing that ever happened in his life. He could feel freedom in his bones, just by having on the blue cloth.

Has Frederick Douglass made any speeches in your area? He has been all around the country challenging young men to join the army and get at the throat of treason and slavery. Douglass was quoted as saying, "It is better even to die free, than to live like slaves."

The slaves have so much to lose if this war isn't won.

As usual I am rambling on, but there doesn't seem to be any news except the war and its effects. All the family here are well, except for a few minor colds.

I hope you and your family are keeping safe and warm.

Stitching for others,

Maggie

Thursday, February 26, 1863
Franklin, Kansas

Dear Caroline,

Please forgive me for writing another black letter.

The Pieratt family has had a double blow of tragedy hit them. Death seems to stalk this family. I mourn along with them, because Robert and Nancy were an extension of our own.

Robert died at Fort Scott on February 19. He had the measles, then succumbed to pneumonia. We barely knew he was sick until Mr. Pieratt got word that he was dead and buried.

I curse this war! If it hadn't been for the Secession, Robert would have been home, alive and well. I can't stand to think what conditions Robert lived in and must have died in without his family around him in his last hours. In my mind I picture him lying in a spindly cot without enough blankets, no one to bathe his fevered brow, all alone. Did he still have my quilt with him? Did he lose it, or wasn't it thick enough to keep him warm and safe? Questions keep haunting me, along with his friendly face. I saw it only two months ago!

I've known him for five years. We climbed the Blue Mound together, rode horseback—were best friends and playmates. Robert escorted his sisters and me to wherever we wanted to go. He seemed to understand my awkwardness to adjusting to the prairie life and did not scoff at my struggles.

We were just starting to see each other in a different light when this war separated us. Now I won't ever know if a courtship would have blossomed between us. I still can't imagine never seeing him again.

Caroline, will I always be waiting for his return?

The word of Robert's passing came after his stepmother, Nancy, died of bronchitis on the 20th. She hadn't been well for the last month but turned worse quickly at the end. The Pieratt children have lost two mothers. I feel their pain as I relive my own loss. Life can be so hard on children.

Remember the nightmares I used to have as a child? They returned after Nancy's death. I see our mother reaching for me, but I can't make out her face. Only this time I was at my present age standing in the doorway, with Nancy beside me. No matter which way I turned, death was near.

I worry what this means. I know it does not make sense, but I have a foreboding that I will join these mothers at an early age. I will be despondent over these deaths for some time.

I wish I could have talked to Nancy about death. She didn't fight it at the end. Just one last breath, and she was gone. How did it feel to know that life was slipping away? Was she prepared to meet her Maker? Was she worried about her family, or did she know others would step in, as she had after Deborah Pieratt died?

Lucinda has overworked herself trying to help her sister in Nancy's last hours. I secretly fear for Lucinda's baby, due next month.

I can't stand another death.

Numb with shock of the past and present,

Maggie

Tuesday, June 16, 1863
Franklin, Kansas

Dear Caroline,

Our nephew Asa Dutton Kennedy is growing just as fast as the crops around here. I know he is only two months old, but Asa will be crawling around before we know it. His eyes are starting to follow the antics of his sister, Lizzie, and Mary Pieratt, who seems to be over here half the time now that her mother is gone. It gives Lucinda comfort to take care of her sister's baby, and it gives the Pieratt girls a relief from this busy little child.

Our brother Michael made it safely from Indiana and is staying with us. With such a large amount of work to do with the crops and livestock this summer, he has been kept busy between here and the other Kennedy farms.

I hope he sticks around and doesn't take off for the front. Losing the battle at Fredericksburg last month had people worried until General Grant took Jackson, Mississippi. Let's hope the plan to conquer Vicksburg, Mississippi, and Port Hudson, Louisiana, to control the entire Mississippi River goes as planned this summer.

The border counties from the Kaw River all the way down to Fort Scott have been emptied of settlers because of the guerrilla raids. We've had our share of problems in our county, but luckily nothing more than a few scattered incidents. We don't see the Home Guards out watching the roads as much because we've gotten this far in the war and have not been attacked.

Lawrence is booming with citizens and businesses. The newspaper said it is the second largest city in Kansas now. It will continue to grow once the bridge is completed over the Kaw and the railroad connects us to Wyandotte.

Besides the war supplies being shipped out of the area, we're getting more prospectors traveling through since gold was found in the Montana Territory this month. I don't know if it will be as big a rush, like the Colorado one, but many people want to be the first to find out.

Unfortunately, the price of supplies goes up for us also. Flour has gone from $2.75 to $4.25 for a hundred pounds in the last year. Many neighbors are growing their own tobacco, cotton, flax, sorghum, and hemp this season. Someone said we'll make enough rope to hang all the Rebels this side of the Mississippi River.

I've done my share of hoeing the crop. Every stab I take at a weed goes for the cause, to get this war over with.

I still think of Robert daily. But I have decided it was better to lose him to a disease in a hospital than have him die in slow agony from wounds while abandoned on a battlefield.

Yes, I'm still having morbid thoughts. I can't help it with all the newspaper articles about the war and the misery it is causing. Can you imagine living in caves and surviving on mule meat? That's what the women and children were doing in Vicksburg, Mississippi, while the two sides were fighting. Why can't the Rebels see what they are doing to their families and give up?

I better finish this letter and deliver it to the post office before I go over to Pieratt's store. I promised to help behind the store counter this afternoon because Mr. Pieratt and James Monroe are busy with field work.

Mercantiling seems to come natural to me. Could it be because I spent my crawling years in our parent's store? I'm just glad I can help out.

Hope all is well in Ohio.

Keeping busy in Kansas,

Maggie

Monday, August 3, 1863
Franklin, Kansas

Dear Caroline,

I'm taking a few quick moments to write. The last of the washed clothes are now on the line. I imagine they will be dry before I get this letter done.

Two weeks ago it was hot enough to boil a turkey! Then we had cool air move in from the north, but it was full of smoke. For three days we had a low-hanging blanket of haze that was coming from fires in the drought-stricken areas in Iowa and Minnesota. It cleared after the wind shifted. Now we're back to steaming humidity and soaring temperatures. Crops, jobs, and war losses are all increasing with the heat.

Lucinda bought some of those new patent fruit jars and we've been filling them with the black thimbleberries that are so abundant now. The Pieratt girls and I scoured the Wakarusa banks for wild grapes last week. They were thick this year with such good weather. It's a lot of work now, but we'll enjoy our cellar full of fruit delicacies this winter.

Agriculture of all kinds is keeping the state busy. Lawrence's Cotton Convention earlier this summer brought the farmers, and skeptics, out to view the new crop being tried in the area. One farmer along the Wakarusa planted 200 acres this spring. Stands of the cotton were poor for those who tried it. An experienced Southern farmer said it was because of the cool wet spell we had this spring. But there is a market for cotton if it can be harvested and ginned.

The war has become a main source of income for the Kansas farmers. Farmers are boasting that these are the best crops they have ever had here. Oats topped fifty bushels to the acre. Food is being shipped out by thousands of teamsters and animals heading for forts, western trading posts, and the armies in the East.

Our neighbors plan to drive livestock together to the forts next week. Fort Scott just let out a contract for beef at $4.97 a head. Advertisements in the *Kansas State Journal* are calling for

500 mules and 200 harness-broke horses to be brought up to Fort Leavenworth. Anyone with a skill, from building a wagon to driving one can have a job. Sales in the stores are brisk and money is pouring in.

Thousands of Negroes are moving into the state. The colored population from western Missouri has shifted to eastern Kansas. It is not uncommon to see fifty to a hundred at a time passing through Franklin. They are a happy lot, singing and laughing with joy for their newfound freedom.

At first the slaves were liberated by General Lane and others who made raids across the border. Now they are boldly "stealing" themselves in neighborhood groups, often with their master's horses, buggies, and belongings in tow. In many cases they are bringing more household goods into the state than the first settlers did.

Last winter the slaves were fleeing over the frozen Missouri River north of Kansas City. This summer most of the groups are crossing the border anywhere they can along the state lines. Even though the opportunity is there, some aren't taking employment because slavery and work mean the same thing to them. But we have several employed in our area and they seem to be good workers. Most Kansans still think the former slaves are inferior and regard them with amusement and distrustful fear. I imagine it will take time for both sides to adjust.

At least they are not Seceshes, or maybe you call them copperheads in Ohio. Kansas has no tolerance for traitors. People traveling through the state soon find out we are for the Union here.

Lawrence got up in arms last week because there was a rumor that Quantrill was going to raid. The town relaxed after he didn't show up in a few days.

Many family members of the guerrillas on the Missouri border have been shipped off to Arkansas or jailed to keep them from supplying their men with food. The government hopes the men will move to be with their families. Camps of well-armed troops have been posted about every 12 miles along the border to keep small raiding parties from entering. Being cavalry they could alert the state if larger bands crossed the line to invade the state.

In the meanwhile, the Red Legs (men with red-leather leggings) keep showing up with horses to sell in Lawrence. I've heard they are molesting proslavers, probably on both sides of the border, stealing their animals and household goods, and bringing them back to Douglas County. They are keeping the vicious circle of bitterness and resentment between Kansas and Missouri going.

Soldiers—white, black, and red—continue to congregate and drill in the county. The other day some Kaw Indian soldiers went through the area. They were a sight because they only had on their new drawers! Because of the heat they left off their uniforms. I wish I could do the same!

James Monroe Pieratt gave me a painted ivory fan for my seventeenth birthday last month. He also gave me a kiss on the cheek. He escorted me to the Mabie's Grand Menagerie last week when the circus came to town. (If the performers risk the problems of the times, we at least should patronize their shows!) And I'm going with him to the Promenade Concert at the Eldridge House tomorrow night.

Our brothers have been teasing me that James Monroe is sweet on me. We have been together quite a bit this summer, but that is because of the family gatherings, and my working at their store.

Confidentially, James Monroe is handsome, and I love the attention he gives me, whatever his intentions are.

From hot and bustling Douglas County,

Maggie

Friday, August 28, 1863
Franklin, Kansas

Dear Caroline,

It is early morning. The birds are slowly adding their waking calls to the cool morning breeze. A patch of orange pink is starting to hint at a sunrise. The western sky is still dark with the leftovers of night. It is so calm and peaceful, just as it was last Friday, before . . .

I couldn't sleep, so I rose early to pen this letter. I thought I better write to assure you that the family survived the brutal attack on Lawrence and the surrounding countryside. I'm sure by now you have heard of the terrible massacre last Friday by Quantrill and his followers.

Cousin Bridge was in town that day. Even though he was unarmed, he escaped injury. He put out the fires that were started. William James and John Alonzo entered town from the north on the ferry after the deed, helped in the chase for about ten miles, but then turned back to the ruined town.

Most of the surrounding community have been in Lawrence to help the survivors this week. Tents, clothing, bedding, and food have been donated by surrounding towns. I gave dresses and linen from my hope chest to people I knew in Lawrence. I still can't believe some of my friends and their fathers are gone.

There had been rumors of a raid, but they had passed without any result. Because of the ordinance in Lawrence forbidding arms to be carried in town, weapons were locked up in the armory and people went about their business because the rumors never materialized.

Now we hear that late on the afternoon of the 20th, a huge group of riders passed over the state line from Missouri within sight of the military camp near Aubry. Although the whole camp saw them, the captain there only sent word to the other military camps to the north and south, but not west to warn the interior towns. They were confused because many of the riders wore the blue shirts of the Union.

45

The column of riders continued to push on without being questioned. To find their way through the dark moonless night they picked up farmers along the way to show them the trail. When the guides were no longer sure of the road they were shot, and then another guide was picked up at the next farmhouse.

They headed straight down the California Road that goes from Westport and crosses the Wakarusa at Bluejacket's Ford.

They passed through Franklin by the first glimmer of day. Someone just getting up counted a hundred columns of four horseman each, with extras mixed in. The call to hurry up and not stop because they were an hour behind time was heard. It was later found out that Dr. Williams was on Quantrill's death list because he was a juror in a trial involving this man's crimes some years ago. It is chilling to think that they passed right by his door and could have murdered him. August 21 was his birth date. Can you imagine having your loved one killed on his birthday?

Franklin could have had the same fate as Lawrence.

The guerrillas broke into a gallop and quickly covered the five miles to Lawrence. They paused to look upon the sleeping town, then rushed in to change its history forever. The 450 horsemen dashed into town, shooting into house windows and at every man that ventured out to see what was going on.

First thing they did was hit an encampment of new recruits and a nearby colored soldier camp. The boys were shot and trampled in their tents before they could rise. The Union flag that flew above one camp was tied to a guerrilla's horsetail and dragged to shreds along the streets.

The group split to cut off anyone escaping from the east or west sides of town, and the rest went up Massachusetts Street. Arriving at the river, they cut the cables to the ferry, sealing off any help that might have attempted to rescue the town. The new bridge over the river isn't finished yet, so it was useless.

After pillaging the rooms of the Eldridge House and terrorizing its guests, the guerrillas set the building on fire. Proceeding down the streets, the raiders broke into the houses, throwing out the loot they wanted, breaking and piling up what they didn't want, and lighting a match to the heap to the horror of the awakened family.

Over 150 men were shot dead and many more left wounded. It didn't matter if they were young or old, clutching a child in their arms or running down the street. Blasts of bullets hailed upon them until they were down. The screaming wives were not permitted to pull their dead husbands out of the doors of the burning houses.

After they destroyed the houses, they emptied both the banks and the liquor shops, then plundered and burned the business district along Massachusetts Street.

The trauma lasted four hours. Before long a huge column of smoke rose above the town. The air was so still that the smoke rose straight upward. It could be seen from thirty miles away.

At nine o'clock the group reassembled and left. They headed south, burning farmsteads along the way. They crossed at Blanton's Bridge, going very near Cousin Bridge's place. Brooklyn was set alight. Baldwin was spared because neighbors of Lawrence and Union troops from the border camps were finally on their trail by this time. Many of the packhorses loaded with plunder were abandoned near the southern Douglas County line.

The soldiers almost caught up with the guerrillas once, but Quantrill turned on them and forced them back. The troop horses were collapsing, tired of traveling all night, so the exhausted soldiers quit the chase. The troops were accused of escorting Quantrill's followers out of Kansas instead of catching them. The poor soldiers probably were afraid to take them on because they would have been cut to pieces by the ruthless killers.

The soldiers resumed their search the next morning, but the guerrillas had scattered into the Missouri hills. During this last week about a hundred raiders have been killed, but Quantrill and his leaders have eluded capture.

The murderers told the Lawrence survivors that the raid was done in revenge for what Lane, Jennison, and other Jayhawkers had done to their families and Missouri properties in the past. The final straw was when some of their women, including sisters of the notorious guerrilla Bill Anderson were jailed in Kansas City waiting their exile South. The old building where they were being held collapsed, killing and injuring most of the women.

After that, the guerrillas plotted the ultimate retaliation—to destroy Lawrence, the prospering abolitionist town.

We could see the fire in the western sky as morning rose. It starting with a few wisps, then grew wider and blacker as it got out of control. Alarm grew because pickets were stationed around the town, preventing anyone from entering to help put out the fires. We knew then that Lawrence was under attack.

Our neighbors gathered, armed with weapons of any kind, ready to fight the intruders, which eventually had to leave the town and travel back to Missouri. We didn't know which route they would take and whether we would be in their path. After we heard the guerrillas had left, we entered Lawrence to see what had happened. We went to help the victims, but the shock made me retch and almost faint.

I had no sense of time as I wandered through the town. The whole city was affected. There were trails of blackened blood in the dusty streets where men staggered and fell. Bodies were piled up in the streets, on sidewalks, among the gardens—black charred trunks without limbs. There was a woman sitting amid the ashes of her home, hugging her husband's blackened skull. People were in shock beyond crying. More than 200 homes and stores were destroyed.

Quantrill had told his men they would be shot themselves if they abused women or children during this raid. What did Quantrill think he was saving them for? The victims' families will be forever haunted with these images.

We washed the faces of the wounded and tried to shade them from the scorching sun. There was a doctor who survived the ordeal, but his office, tools, and medicines had been destroyed, making it hard for him to patch the wounded until supplies arrived from other towns.

The Methodist church was set up as morgue. Women, severely burned and bloodied from the ordeal, came in to identify their husbands. Most of them lost their husbands, sons, houses, and businesses that morning. All they had to their names was the clothing they were wearing at 5 o'clock in the morning.

All the coffins in town had been destroyed, or the carpenters were dead, so a hundred coffins were brought from Leavenworth.

Most of the dead were buried by the next day because of the heat. Some remains were put in mass graves on top of Mount Oread. There was an eerie glow capping the sky above the town that night. Basements were still radiating like furnaces, with bones showing among the embers. Church services last Sunday were only prayers for the dead, no singing or preaching.

People panicked later that Sunday when someone mistook a trash fire outside of town for the return of the guerrillas. Families spent the night huddled in outlying fields during one of the coldest, most severe thunderstorms we have had in years.

I still shudder with horror when the carnage flashes in my mind. I'll be fine, and then I'll hear the forlorn cry of a baby, see the bloodstained mother holding what is left of her husband's body, smell the burning wood and flesh. The scenes of Black Friday will always be with me.

How can men pump bullets into unarmed people, steal property that has taken a lifetime to build, and then set fire to buildings knowing there are still human beings alive in them? Oh, Caroline. Now I realize what war is. It's brutal, cold-blooded, and a constant nightmare for the families left behind.

Would I have had the courage to cling desperately to the reins of a plunging horse to deter the ruffian's aim? Could I have battled flames and searing heat to save men trapped in burning buildings?

I'm still filled with horror when I think that if those men had taken a different route, it could have been me trying to shield our brothers from death. It could have been me standing beside a cellar full of burning timbers.

It could have happened to me.

In shock and sadness,

Maggie

Thursday, September 24, 1863
Franklin, Kansas

Dear Caroline,

Things were still in turmoil weeks after the raid. General Lane (who escaped Quantrill's hunt by hiding in a cornfield), had been giving talks in Lawrence and Leavenworth to thousands of people, trying to get the citizens to raid and scorch Missouri, to "turn it into a desert." A few hundred did meet at Paola as planned on September 8, but they ended up spending the day listening to speeches in a driving rain. The government forbade anyone to cross the borders and, luckily, most people were levelheaded enough to realize that these raids have got to stop in order to end the violence. Many think that Lane, and the problems he has stirred up during the past three years, are more to blame for the Lawrence raid than Quantrill himself.

For the first time since the war started, the Kansas Militia is finally equipped. Eight thousand stands of arms were shipped to the state. Every portion of the border will be protected by companies of men because Quantrill and most of his band were never caught. About half of the population of Lawrence, mostly widows and children, have traveled back to their families in the East. They lost all their money and belongings and had no means—or heart—to start over.

Rubble is being cleared away and rebuilding is starting. The sounds of hammers and saws echo into the countryside. Stores are slowly reopening (temporarily in a tent or a corncrib) as merchandise is being shipped in again. Money, food, and supplies from the East and area towns have been sent for the needy. With bolts of cloth sent here, women have been sewing clothing and bedding to give to the bereaved families. I think I've sewn more pairs of underwear and petticoats in the past month than I had in my entire lifetime before.

We've found out how much the innocent residents of western Missouri have been affected by all this, too.

Four days after the raid, Order Number 11 was issued by General Ewing, stating that all people in the border counties of

Missouri between the Missouri and Osage Rivers must evacuate their land in fifteen days. If they weren't gone by September 9, they would be considered Rebels and dealt with accordingly. The families had to go to the military station nearest them to establish their Union loyalty, and then move to the station or into Kansas. This needed to be done in order to prevent further raids on both sides of the border and to calm the people of Kansas. All food, shelter, grains, and livestock not taken off the farms was to be destroyed so it would not feed the guerrillas still on the loose.

Mr. Pieratt's brother and family lived in Cass County, Missouri. The two families came together from Kentucky in '54, but John traveled on to Kansas, while his brother, James, stayed in Missouri with his wife's family. The family—James, Mary, and their five boys ages seventeen to ten, and Mary's sister, Nellie Tipton—showed up at John Pieratt's farm during the middle of this month. They had nowhere else to go. It wasn't safe, nor did they have money to travel Back East. They arrived with less than when they had left Kentucky nine years ago.

The stories they told, Caroline. I had no idea how bad these raids were in Missouri until I heard firsthand.

After the war started, Red Legs and soldiers from our side raided their area just because they were in Missouri. The guerrillas also came through, looting food and terrorizing them for being Union. Outbuildings were torched, furniture smashed, livestock stolen, sometimes by people they had known from years past. Most of their valuables and stored grains were gone long before Order Number 11. They had paid for that acreage, built a homestead, planted crops to eat and sell, lived there for years— and then had to abandon it all.

And their evacuation was just as bad. Streams of people were leaving at once, most of their few belongings hastily stashed in broken-down wagons. All Pieratts' horses were taken, and they were left with an old mule and cow to pull their scant load.

Ewing's men, watching the evacuation, asked if they were Union or Secesh, but an answer of Union didn't make much difference because they were still "Missourian." Having a Loyalty Oath certificate didn't matter to some soldiers, who searched the wagons for weapons and harassed the people mercilessly.

Soldiers pilfered the Pieratts' things, stacking coverlets and clothing on their own horses. Some troops didn't wait for the families to clear off their land before setting their homes on fire. This was happening days before the deadline. To protest meant a beating or death.

James Pieratt, although too old to be enlisted as a soldier, was in extra peril, being an able-bodied man. It is a wonder that he and the older boys made it through the turmoil alive. Many didn't. Most groups were families without husbands or fathers along.

James and Mary Pieratt are resigned to the circumstances, but their older boys are full of animosity and the youngest is frightened. Nellie seems to be dealing with the trauma the best. Maybe it is because she had the least to lose, being unmarried and in her late fifties.

James and the two oldest, Jimmy and Albert, got jobs immediately. Will, Johnny, and Val are helping around the Pieratt farm. Nellie took over the kitchen, which was fine with the Pieratt girls, who have had the whole responsibility this past year.

We're helping Mary replenish their bedding before the winter cold sets in. She had tucked a few quilt blocks in a pillow case when they left Missouri. I took them home to make more and sew them together. One is the Missouri Star, a geometric composition that requires concentration. She also had five Churn Dash blocks, a pretty four-patch design that will go together quickly.

As you can tell by my letter, our fall is being taken up with helping others. But I'm glad I'm here to help and not on the receiving end.

Sheltering and clothing others,

Maggie

Thursday, November 26, 1863
Franklin, Kansas

Dear Caroline,

President Lincoln has declared today, the fourth Thursday in November, to be a national day of Thanksgiving. I hardly see reason to give thanks with all the problems in our state and nation. But perhaps we should just be grateful to be alive, to have the right to speak and print what we want, to come and go as we please. Although this war is horrible, we should be thankful that it is giving four million more people these same rights.

This fall continues to be a constant stress to us. There is a fifty-mile strip of empty desolate prairie along the borders because Quantrill released an issue saying he was going to raid Kansas again. All companies of the state militia practice their drills on Saturday afternoons if they are not already on patrol. Sightings of Quantrill since September have pushed the militia to the state of exhaustion as they chase all over two states trying to find him. Fields have gone unharvested because the men are gone from home. Once again the women are left to fend for themselves.

Last month General Blunt's staff was attacked by Quantrill and several hundred guerrillas near Baxter Springs, which is in the far southeast corner of our state. The group killed over eighty men and also attacked the small post of Fort Blair.

At this rate we're going to run out of able men to fight the enemy. It is getting hard for the Union to find soldiers because so many have already served time in the war or are too old. Besides the Union offering a $300 bounty if a man volunteers for three years of service, they are trying to get slaves from border states to enlist if they have their owners' permission. Some young men of means are paying $300 for substitutes to take their place.

People here are disillusioned with the war. They were willing to fight for the Union in the beginning but now just want the war to end and don't really care which side wins. The cost of living has risen so high and the South is starving. How is that going to help our nation?

The owner of the *Kansas State Journal* starting printing the newspaper again last month. It's a small hand-press edition because the office and printing press were destroyed in the raid. Before the town's destruction, the newspaper was full of store ads. Now there are only accounts of Quantrill's raid and war news.

The telegraph line to Lawrence was finished last month, so we know about the fighting in Tennessee that has dragged on for months. We pray that Grant will finally win that campaign.

We heard about President Lincoln dedicating a soldiers' cemetery at Gettysburg, Pennsylvania, last week. Last July, when I read about the battle at Gettysburg that killed over 10,000 soldiers, I couldn't fathom thousands of men and horses littering the countryside. But after seeing the destruction of Lawrence, I knew exactly how it looked.

Christmas will be upon us soon, but with no joy or celebrations. There are no theaters left standing, no social halls to hold holiday parties in, and no one in the mood anyway.

I will be thinking of you, dear sister, and I pray you will be thinking of us. I cannot wish you a happy New Year because I'm afraid one is not looming in our future next year.

Sending love to all,

Maggie

Pledging the Union

Wednesday, April 6, 1864
Franklin, Kansas

Dear Caroline,

The James Pieratt family left for California this week. Having little left to their name, they decided to pack their meager belongings and head west to start over again. After painful consideration they decided not to try to reclaim their Missouri farm, because it could mean years of waiting before they could go back. I'm sure they would have to start over from scratch, for there would be nothing but burned rubble left.

They wanted to get away from the war and escape its problems. The oldest boys were of age to be drafted into the army, so they decided to clear out before this happened because the war continues to escalate.

It will take months of travel on the California Road to reach their destination. At least they won't be the first. Many have made the trip in the past two decades, so there is a marked trail and trading posts along the way.

Making one long overland journey in the past helped them pack for this one. They acquired two study wagons, strong oxen to pull them, and livestock to herd to their new home. The wagons were stuffed with new bedding, clothing, cooking utensils, and a few household items they were able to salvage from Missouri. They did not want for food after we offered provisions from our cellars.

One of the few treasures they were able to save from their plight in Missouri was James's fiddle. When they first arrived in Kansas it took Mr. Pieratt a while to play it because of his depression. But Sarah Pieratt begged him to pluck some of the tunes she remembered on the trail from Kentucky. Once he got started, the tunes and memories of their trip flowed out of all of them. I spent hours listening to their funny and harrowing stories.

They asked John Pieratt if he wanted to join their trek, but he is making a good living with the store and farm and did not want to leave Kansas.

I was glad that was his decision, because I didn't want to move to California and leave my Kennedy family. You see, James Monroe Pieratt and I have become engaged. We have not set a wedding date yet, though. I want to get married and start a family of my own, but at the same time I'm hesitant because of the war. What if James gets drafted and killed in a battle? I'd be a young widow, probably with children to worry about.

Friends say to go ahead and enjoy wedded life while I can and not worry about the uncertain future. William James said he would give me his consent, since I am underage. What do you think I should do?

My other concern is the lack of items in my hope chest. The circumstances of others this past year has taken my supply of bedding and linens to almost nothing. I'm thinking we should wait until winter to marry so I can remake my trousseau. Aunt Margaret said to go ahead and get married this summer. (I was shocked when she said I wouldn't need much on a warm night with a new husband anyway!) She offered to contribute to my bedding needs this fall after harvest is done.

In the meantime Quantrill is back raiding the country after wintering in Texas. Even with the border guard in place, people have the feeling that he can cross the state line and hit our cities again. Most people keep a sack of indispensable clothing packed and ready to grab if we need to take flight.

What will it take to end this nightmare?

Trying to decide my future,

Maggie

Monday, June 27, 1864
Franklin, Kansas

Dear Caroline,

I'm a married woman! James Monroe and I tied the knot at William James's house last Thursday. It was a simple ceremony using the minister from our church, and the immediate family attending.

I wore my good gray dress and held a nosegay of flowers picked from the patch by the back door. James Monroe wore his best suit—with his revolver in his waistband. My betrothed slid a slim gold band on my finger and the preacher announced we were legally married.

After everyone got a piece of wedding cake, we opened gifts from family and friends. Everything from produce to silverware was greatly appreciated. Thank you for your gift of beautiful embroidered linens. It arrived a week before the wedding and is already in use.

Aunt Margaret gave me a small sack of coins to tuck away for emergencies. The shiny coins were brand new from the U.S. Mint and were stamped with "In God We Trust" on the front. That's the first I had seen like that. I hid them in my sewing basket for safekeeping.

After the wedding dinner we moved my belongings the few miles to our new home. James Monroe had been farming on land adjacent to his father's, so we're close to family, but our homestead is south of the Wakarusa, where John's is on the north side. The house is nothing more than a simple shack, but it's all ours!

There was a bouquet of wildflowers on the table to greet me. James Monroe is so thoughtful. Earlier this spring I had dug up perennial roots like yarrow, roses, and coneflowers from the plains and planted them by the house's front stoop. The fruit of my efforts graced my table on my wedding day.

My trunks of bedding and clothing filled the corner of our bedroom. The few dishes and pans I have are now handy on the shelves my husband built on the wall beside the woodstove. Glassware we received as wedding gifts and a small tintype of my parents grace our fireplace mantel. It didn't take long to place my special treasures around the two rooms, but it certainly spruced up James Monroe's bachelor dwelling. I have plans to stitch gingham into curtains and braid rags into rugs before long. I got the new Prairie Star quilt done in time to use on our bed. I used up all the tiny leftover scraps from this year's projects to make a colorful cover.

I'm adjusting to it being just the two of us instead of several extras and children underfoot, as it was at William James's house. I'm having a hard time cooking for two instead of a tableful. Being alone has been good for us to get to know each other better as man and wife. I'm sure I seem shy, but being this close takes time to get used to.

I pray that James Monroe will be able to stay on the farm and not be called out in the militia this year. The situation has been relatively calm in Douglas County so far this summer, but Indian problems have been increasing in western Kansas since several hundred Cheyennes attacked the First Colorado Calvary near Fort Larned in late April.

Denver panicked this month with the Indian uprisings. Women gathered in the U.S. Mint, the brick building in town, but no Indians attacked. The Indians have been taking their revenge on the stage stations along the South Platte River route, though.

We have not heard from the Pieratts since they left for California. Nellie promised to write, but Sarah said that no letters have shown up yet. I hope they got through the problem areas before the Indians started their turmoil. It will take months for them to reach their destination, but we hope to hear from them a few times before, and after, they arrive.

Well, I just wanted to let you know your little sister tied the knot and is now considered a matron!

Yours very truly,

Mrs. James Monroe Pieratt

Tuesday, August 16, 1864
Franklin, Kansas

Dear Caroline,

It is just as I feared. I am alone, and I don't know for how long. We were together barely six weeks when James Monroe was mustered into service August 3. It is supposed to be for a thirty-day period to guard the border, but it is hard to tell when (yes, I will say when, not "if") he comes back.

The Confederate armies continue to gain strength with the arms, clothing, and artillery they captured in the Louisiana, Indian Territory, and Arkansas campaigns. General Sterling Price's troops have grown to 20,000 soldiers. Union forces are concentrating in Little Rock, Arkansas, and Fort Smith.

Almost all of the Kennedy, Pieratt, and Shields men—brothers, brothers-in-law, cousins, and sons—were mustered into the Third Regiment of the Kansas State Militia in August.

I tried to be brave and not show fear as he was getting ready to leave. I packed his haversack with the needed supplies—a tin plate, cup, and silverware. I teased him I was going along in his bag. He was adamant I wasn't going to be a tagalong camp follower until I handed him his "housewife," the soldiers' nickname for their sewing kits.

I made sure he carried along a supply of biscuits, molasses cookies, and dried meat. The government should be supplying his food, but I wanted to be sure he started out with decent nourishment. Because he has to carry everything, he has to limit the weight. It won't last but a portion of his trip, but that way he won't have to buy from sulters, the wagon merchants, right away.

The last thing he picked up before going out the door was his little Bible. He tried to slip it in his pocket without me seeing it, but I wasn't spared the dreadful thought that went with the action. Soldiers usually carry a Bible with their names in it. That way, if they are killed in action, this book will be taken out of their pockets and left on their chests to identify them to the people burying the dead.

I did not send a hair ribbon this time.

Being alone has been exhausting. It is so lonely at night that I hear every noise within a mile. If the dogs bark, I am instantly awake. It doesn't help that the heat has been suffocating this month.

I miss falling asleep in the curve of James Monroe's arms. Instead, I'm tucked in bed with the pistol under his pillow and a shaker of red pepper on my bedside table. Now I know what it was like for the women during the Bleeding Kansas years.

Meantime the crops and livestock must be taken care of. Harvest of the fall crops is only a short time away. I panic to think my husband might not be back in time to take over. We were counting on help from family men to get the corn picked. What will I do if none of them are back in time?

I'm spending most of my time in the garden. We had a dry spring, but rains were good since July, producing a bumper crop in the garden that James Monroe planted for me last spring. This morning I spent sweating in the garden, picking a big mess of beans to preserve. The patch got away from me because I haven't felt well from the heat and worry, so there is extra catch-up work to do this week. Both Lucinda and Aunt Margaret asked me to come live with them during this month, but I am determined to take care of the place in James Monroe's absence.

Lucinda has been over once, but William James is gone also, so she needs to be home. She has help—or more trouble, I haven't decided which. They have a young former slave staying with them now. Ann, only fifteen, was still in shock when William James brought her home. She doesn't know the whereabouts of her parents, who were separated from her and sold. Luckily, Ann was railroaded north to safety. I'd describe her as a scared wild child, not knowing cleanliness or manners. Lucinda must start from scratch to teach her domestic work. Ann can watch over the children by herself but can't fix a decent meal. For her own safety she is not permitted to go far from the house. Her life would be in jeopardy if she were seen by the wrong traveler. I'm sure patient Lucinda will bring the girl around.

Besides the war and border problems, full-scale Indian war broke out last month in the state. Kiowas, Arapahoes, and Comanches are roaming up and down the Santa Fe Trail from

Cimarron to Council Grove robbing stations and ranches, stealing horses, and killing people. They have also attacked settlers this month near Marysville and Clay Center, which is northwest of Lawrence. These problems have interrupted the mail between here and the west. Just to get a letter to and from Colorado, it has to go by way of the Pacific Coast and Panama. Halting the supply trains going west will cause prices to soar and starvation to loom in the future for people caught along the trails.

So I sit here by myself, with no word from James Monroe in the East, or his family in the West. Please write, and tell Mary Ann to do the same.

And please don't worry. If news of another raid hits the county, I'll be one of the first to flee to shelter. I'm not that sentimental about our little shack!

From the lonely bride,

Maggie

Tuesday, September 20, 1864
Franklin, Kansas

Dear Caroline,

James Monroe returned home the end of August, luckily all in one piece save his extra shirt and his silverware. I was glad to part with a few household items to have him back safely.

We were cheered that the Union and General Sherman took possession of Atlanta the first of this month. With our invincible Union Navy you would think that the close of the war must be near ahead. But then there have been rumors of a northward move by General Price from his station in Arkansas. He sounds determined to make one final effort for the Confederate cause in Missouri.

People are starting to panic again because there are few Kansas troops left on our eastern border at the moment. Most of them are fighting Indians in the west. Last week a large Union supply train was attacked and burned at Cabin Creek, in the Cherokee Nation. Meantime our state government tries to keep functioning. Cousin Joe Kennedy was elected as a delegate for the Wakarusa district in our September 8th election. He will be a part of the Kansas Legislature in next year's session.

I've mentioned that former slaves have been moving into the state in droves this past year. Now we have a pair living with us. When James Monroe was coming back from the border, he passed a group on the Westport Road. He didn't give them a second glance until he heard one older black man laugh. It sounded so familiar that he pulled back and returned to the travelers. James Monroe asked the man where he was from, and he said Owingsville, Kentucky.

Come to find out he had been a slave on James Monroe's Grandfather Goodpaster's farm in that area. Even though James Monroe was only ten when he left Kentucky, he recognized the man's unusual voice. "Uncle Ned" as they always called him, and his wife, "Aunt Polly," had taken off west this spring. They had hoped to find family in Missouri but found wasteland instead, prompting them to continue to Kansas.

My father-in-law was so surprised to see them. The situation was a little tense at first, because John had been the master's son-in-law and Uncle Ned the slave, but since then they have spent hours talking about the family back home in Kentucky—the changes in the county, what the war has done to the area, what neighbors were still around. I think it has helped John to hear about family again.

John wasn't surprised that his family had split over the war. When he left in '54 some still had slaves and others had set them free, as he had. He was saddened to hear that his nephews and cousins were fighting on opposite sides, though. One cousin fighting for the Rebel side was killed in the Ivy Mountain Battle in Kentucky in '61. Deborah Pieratt's brothers are fighting with the 7th Union Kentucky Calvary there. Uncle Ned didn't know if they were still alive.

John wondered out loud how his children would have been affected by the war if they had stayed in Kentucky. I'm sure he was thinking of Robert, but there is no rhyme or reason why some soldiers live and others die.

For now, Uncle Ned and Aunt Polly have set up their tent in the shade of the Wakarusa banks very near where Deborah and her sister, Ann, are buried. I thought they would be superstitious about staying so close to the graves, but Uncle Ned said it was fine, because he had some catching up to do with his old master's daughters.

I'm not sure Aunt Polly thought the same. She is a quiet woman but is slowly opening up as she gets to know me. I took an interest in her sewing, which seemed to break the barrier. Being proud of her new freedom, she was starting a Union Star quilt. I gave her some blue material to make it look more authentic than just red and white calico and gingham patches. Aunt Polly was so touched that I think we might become friends after all.

Visiting with Kentucky "relatives,"

Maggie

Monday, October 10, 1864
Franklin, Kansas

Dear Caroline,

Our worst nightmare has begun. They are all gone—husbands, brothers, cousins, neighbors—even Uncle Ned. Sixteen thousand Kansas men are running toward our threatened border.

Saturday bells rang and the cannon fired to summon a citizens' defense rally. Governor Carney called out all men of Kansas for immediate report. General Curtis went a step further and placed the whole state under martial law. He directed all men, white and black, between the ages of eighteen and sixty to join the military organization.

All business have halted throughout the state. We're in the middle of fall harvest, but it may end up rotting in the fields. We hardly had time to gather necessities for the mens' departure. Most men just dropped their work, grabbed their weapons, and left on a run, hardly taking time to say good-bye to their families. Only the very young or old men are left as home guards. The main protection for the Kansas interior falls on the shoulders of the women.

Can you imagine the panic this is causing? It means that the Rebels are almost upon us again. If the Confederates get over our border, all may be lost.

General Price started moving westward with his Confederate forces on October 2. His plan is to strike St. Louis, Jefferson City, march up the Missouri River to Kansas City, then on down through Kansas and into the Indian Territory. Recruits, plunder, and destruction of the Union Army installations are his goals.

He also gave the guerrillas free rein to "help out" any way they can. Bloody Bill Anderson, a Quantrill follower, robbed a train and killed many Union soldiers in Centralia, Missouri on September 27. These killers have turned even more ruthless, which means we might not have anything, not even our lives, left by next month.

This weekend I have felt the panic of the war, knowing that the parting with my husband and brothers could have been our final farewells to one another. The worry is suffocating at times, my heart pounds to the point that I feel I will faint with fear. Thoughts of doom come at my first waking moment as the suspense and anxiety refill my mind after a restless night. In some ways I dread facing another day, because although it could mean the end of the war, it could also mean the final battle for so many I know.

I am completely terrified that I will never see James Monroe again. What will I do if he does not return home? And it is not just me to worry about anymore. I am with child. What if James Monroe never makes it home to see his son or daughter? I am anxious enough about childbirth and now I have this fear piled on top.

Aunt Polly and I are going to town to glean any news we can on the men's whereabouts. Maybe there will be news from the border to ease my mind. I hope the War Department has not had to post a tally of killed and wounded soldiers yet. I will faint dead away if I see a Pieratt or Kennedy name on the list.

I must stop my fretful letter and mail it. I hope it can get through to you. Keep us all in your prayers.

Anxiously dreading the worst,

Maggie

Thursday, November 3, 1864
Franklin, Kansas

Dear Caroline,

I thank God that I can report that James Monroe and our brothers are home again! James Monroe came in the door a few days ago looking his worst in his shabby, mud-splattered clothes. I tried to show that I had been brave during his absence, but I cried like a baby once I was in his arms again. He about did the same when he realized he was safely home.

James Monroe gave me an account of his absence with only brief answers to my questions at first. Slowly, after hours of sleep and nourishment, he opened up and talked. Tears came to his eyes more than once as he told of the battles he was forced to experience.

We women knew they were stationed at Olathe at first, but the water was bad there so 10,000 men were moved on to Shawneetown. Days passed and Price didn't show up. It turned out that St. Louis and Jefferson City were too well garrisoned for the Confederates to take over, so they moved on to Boonville for several days. Meanwhile, the men on the border wanted to go back home because there was no sight of the Rebels. And they didn't want to cross into Missouri to find them either. By the 20th it was decided that the danger of invasion ceased to exist, if it ever did. Then they got word that a group of 2,000 Kansans that had crossed the border met Price's group of 28,000 at Lexington, Missouri. Our side was forced back to the Little Blue River, east of Independence, by nightfall.

The next morning the Kansas troops were driven farther west to Independence after eight hours of fighting. On the 21st, the Confederate troops pushed across Byron's Ford on the Big Blue. At sundown the Union troops retired to Westport. On the 22nd, the Union troops had fallen back to entrenchments in Kansas City. The battle resumed on the 23rd with charges and counter-charges, hand-to-hand combat, and artillery firing from every point of vantage.

James Monroe was in a trance as he told about men, many he knew, who were shot, lying bleeding with no hope of help until the battle ended. As he talked, his world narrowed back down to the battlefields where there was no escape from the fearful sights of wounded men begging to die, the nightmares in his catnaps between battles, his worry about me at home alone.

James Monroe said soldiers on both sides talked to one another across the picket lines in the evening, trading rations, reporting the results of the latest battle. Under the flag of truce, some men crossed the lines to look for relatives or visit the wounded—only to resume fighting again at dawn.

He tried to keep in sight of the rest of the family, but they were scattered across the fields of battle. His father was in the 21st Regiment while James and the rest were with the 3rd Regiment, although in different companies.

The enemy finally fell back when General Pleasanton's three Union brigades from Jefferson City, Missouri, who had been chasing the Rebels across the state, closed in on the Confederate rear. The retreating Confederate troops crowded into Kansas, entering through Linn County, with their sights on capturing Fort Scott.

The Rebels plundered and burned their way south with the Kansas men in pursuit. The Confederates dropped off stolen cattle and Negroes in haste at Trading Post and took a stand at Mine Creek when their wagon train bogged down. The battles on the 25th on Mine Creek and the Little Osage turned the Confederates back into Missouri, where they were finally defeated at Newtonia. Many Confederate soldiers were taken prisoner.

Finally, exhausted and scattered over the countryside, the Union soldiers returned to Fort Scott and General Price went unpursued. The Kansas men were mustered out on the 27th and made their way back home. General Pleasanton's group followed Price until they were over the Arkansas River. I shuddered when James Monroe said that if Price had captured Fort Leavenworth, which is only thirty miles northwest of Kansas City, then Kansas, Nebraska, and beyond would have fallen under Confederate power.

News of their proximity to us during the battles made everyone in Douglas County ready to flee. Aunt Polly, Lucinda, and I had packed our belongings into one wagon and were prepared to hitch up the fastest horse team to it and head west at a moment's notice.

Unfortunately we did not get through the battles without a loss of immediate family. Lucinda's brother, Robert Shields, in Company H of the 11th Kansas Calvary, lost his life during the first part of October. Thankfully, Robert was recognized and brought back home from the battleground. He was buried in the Franklin Cemetery beside his two young sons who passed before him. His widow, Margaret, is left to carry on the farm and family by herself.

All the cemeteries in the area have fresh mounds of earth in them. I can't recall the number of funerals I've attended in the last three years. For fighting for their country, all the soldiers get is a flag wrapped about their coffin and a military escort to their grave. And how many men have been killed and buried where they fell, never coming back to their home state soil?

It seems as if burial hymns and poems are always haunting my mind. What must be going through the minds of the men fresh from the battlefield?

Thinking of our losses,

Maggie

Tuesday, December 20, 1864
Franklin, Kansas

Dear Caroline,

Yesterday the first train ran between Wyandotte and Lawrence, finally connecting us to the East by rail. In Ohio we took train transportation for granted. Here it was a major achievement to link the line to any big city. You'd think that the President was on the train himself for all the fanfare that went with its arrival.

Maybe the war will be over soon and we could travel to Ohio for a visit next Christmas. I'd love to meet your and Mary Ann's new children and have you meet my new child—and James Monroe, of course. Wouldn't it be something to be together again with all the little ones?

James Monroe thinks the war is close to ending because General Sherman and over 60,000 Union men marched from Atlanta to Savannah, Georgia, and on to the port of Fort McAllister last week. Just about all of the South has been conquered now.

The Kansas men got back from the border in time to vote in the November presidential election. Many Kansans were not happy with Lincoln because he backed General Lane but in the end voted for him to be reelected. There was no alternative if the war is to be concluded, and the South and slavery stopped.

Some Union troops are now heading west to take care of the Indian troubles. They are being reinforced by captured Confederates who have pledged allegiance to the Union. Rations are getting low in prisoner camps, so men have changed sides to get food. I've heard they are scoffed at by Union soldiers because they are considered turncoats who deserted their cause and their comrades. They call them "Galvanized Yankees" because they have a thin coating of Yankeeism, just as iron may have a thin outer layer of zinc.

In some ways the soldiers have made the situation worse in the west instead of better. A troop attacked a Cheyenne-Arapaho village, killing over 500 Indians, last month. The newspaper said there will be a congressional investigation of that massacre. The chief had displayed an American and a white flag to show his peaceful intentions, but it did not save his village. Now other Indians are out attacking way stations and ranches in the eastern part of the Colorado Territory to avenge the army's brutality.

Things are as normal as possible around here. The harvest is finished and the winter supplies laid in for the cold months ahead. I've been baking sugar cookies to hand out to little family members for their Christmas presents. We plan to have a Kennedy holiday meal together this weekend at the new stone schoolhouse over by Aunt Margaret's. It is the only place big enough to hold the whole clan together in one place.

Do you remember the Christmas evening feast Mother used to make? William James and John Alonzo were reminiscing the other day, talking about the stuffed goose, Yorkshire pudding, spiced peaches, and the array of preserves Mother spread on the table. Fine wine was served to the older generation to toast everyone's health. Our best china and glassware was used for the special occasion.

William James had so many childhood memories that I almost felt cheated because I have so few. Of course, he was eighteen when Mother died, while I was four. The only thing I remember was warm gingerbread topped high with whipped cream, and the peppermint stick candy that Father brought home from the store.

James Monroe's childhood Christmas in Kentucky was so different from ours. The whole family would gather in the basement of an inn that his grandparents ran—and more often than not a stranger caught on the road during the holidays joined them at the table. Their feast was an acorn-fattened hog, sweet potatoes swimming in butter, and beignets—a doughnut that their French great-grandfather was fond of—and plenty of ale made in their own still. Their meal was served on tin or pewterware. Molasses taffy was James Monroe's favorite sweet treat.

Uncle Ned's version was a possum and rice supper served on a wooden trencher that was turned over to "the pie side" for a slice of mock apple pie. When asked what they drank, he just laughed and said, "Whatever was handy to reach out of Master's pantry." Uncle Ned and Aunt Polly have added a truly different dimension to my way of thinking. No matter what background a person comes from, we all have the same wants and wishes.

I wish you were with us. The larger my body expands with my little one, the more I think of how important family is. I wonder what our mother dreamed of for the children she was carrying. I have such hopes and plans for this child. It changes your whole way of looking at life, to say the least.

Christmas blessings to you and your family.

Feeling close to you during the holidays,

Maggie

Blanket of Relief

Thursday, March 2, 1865
Franklin, Kansas

Dear Caroline,

I just punched down the bread dough, so I'll start my letter before I need to work it again.

Cousin Salina and Alonzo stopped by yesterday evening. We caught up on family news while the men played checkers and Salina helped me with my latest sewing project. They were in the area to see their new niece and nephew. Ella Alice was born to Nettie and Will on February 19, and Harvey Elmer to Bridge and Elizabeth on the 28th. I haven't had the pleasure of holding either baby yet.

Salina's brother, Joe Kennedy, in Topeka now for the Legislature session, secured a bill to establish and provide a state institution for deaf mutes. You know he helped start the school in Baldwin City when his daughter Matilda started school in '61. Now parents will have state help for their deaf children. Joe and Mary are helping so many others in the state besides their three deaf children.

While Salina was here she helped me stuff my latest quilt. I had saved milkweed silk last fall for filler for my baby coverlet. The silk makes the newborn's cover extra soft and light. I used the Yankee Pride design for the top. Since it is so little, I stitched the back to it and turned it like a pillow case before filling it. The silk was light enough to float off easily. Salina's children were chasing escaped bits around the room as it danced in the air. I'm still finding the little fluff everywhere now that the cabin is bright with morning light.

I've stitched so many dreams into that blanket. Of course I wonder if it will be a boy or a girl, but what will it do when it grows up? Will it live next door or travel to another part of the world? Who will it pick for its mate, how many grandchildren will they give me? What will the baby look like? Will it have my nose or James Monroe's, blue eyes or green? I'm positive it will have a dark thatch of hair like the rest of the Kennedys, although I must admit it could have a red tinge, as John Pieratt has.

As my time draws nearer, I catch myself humming lullabies. Whether rocking and sewing by the fireplace or scattering feed to the chickens, I seem to have a song on my lips. I know the tunes because all the women in our family sing them to their babies. Our mother must have sung the same ones to me nineteen years ago.

Did I tell you that James Monroe's sister, George Ann, married Reuben Moore on the first of January? His family lives a mile west of us, so Reuben watched her grow up. I wouldn't have been ready at age fifteen to get married, but she didn't hesitate when Reuben asked.

Time to get back to the bread. I hope to receive a letter from you soon.

Singing and dreaming while I work,

Maggie

Wednesday, April 12, 1865
Franklin, Kansas

Dear Caroline,

I send a rush of glad tidings your way.

Lawrence (and every other town in Kansas) went wild with relief and exuberance when the townspeople heard that Robert E. Lee had surrendered Richmond, Virginia, to General Grant. Every available flag was waving, bells were clanging, whistles trilling, and there was cheering until people were hoarse. General Lane and former Governor Robinson gave speeches, Old Sacramento was fired, and crowds danced in the streets until the wee hours.

We went into town for the celebration. I thought about staying home because I didn't want to waddle into town in my condition, but this was too important an occasion to miss.

It is such a relief to have the fighting over. Now we can get on with our lives without having to worry about more destruction and loss. Our family survived with minimal loss compared to some who lost all their sons in battles.

I hate to admit it, but my feelings about the end of the war have swung to opposite ends and back again. I'm happy it is over, but I am sad that this war will scar people for life. I have seen so much these past four years that it is hard to be cheerful and not cynical at times. We see more soldiers coming through every day. Some have returned home horribly disfigured, missing arms and legs, blind, deaf, with wounds that aren't healing. They are not well enough to work and far too proud to accept help. How will they and their families survive?

And what about the South? Soldiers passing through the Southern states on their way home say the towns and countryside are in shambles. Everything from bridges to barns was burned down, stands of trees are gone because they were cut for firewood. Southern cattle were driven before the Union troops for meat when it was needed, and all the rest of the food was confiscated or destroyed. All that was left on the plantations are the mansions, standing isolated on the lawns, still holding themselves proud and aloof.

But there were free black soldiers proudly marching down the streets of the Southern towns where they once crouched at their masters' feet. The Confederates' surrender is the Negro's freedom.

I know the destruction had to take place to end the war, but think of the women in those households. Whether we were in log cabins or mansions, we all had to live the terror of the war. I pity the women still waiting for the return of their men and boys. Some will never know what happened to their loved ones.

There had to be some men wounded or killed in the last fight the morning of the surrender. Can you imagine? Think of them going through the whole war, only to lose their lives at the last moment before the end. I hope this country never experiences this kind of hateful destruction again.

I hope all your dear ones and friends are on their ways home from the battlefronts.

Glad the end is here,

Maggie

Saturday, April 29, 1865
Franklin, Kansas

Dear Caroline,

It was such a good feeling to hear that the United States flag was flying over Fort Sumter again. It was exactly four years to the day, April 14, that it had been forced down. Good Friday did seem to be truly that this year.

Think what a relief that was for President Lincoln, the heavy burden of the state of the nation finally lifted from his shoulders. And then the next day the church bells roared, vibrating through the countryside. Even though the ringing slowed down, there was one bell that kept going, ringing one death toll after another. We knew another tragic event had happened by that one ringer.

James Monroe went into town to hear the news. Telegraph keys had spread the report that Lincoln had been shot the night before. Vice President Andrew Johnson was sworn into office the next morning. Our newspaper, edged black, gave the details of the shocking story. The actor, John Wilkes Booth, who shot our President during the play at Ford's Theater had played at Fort Leavenworth, Kansas, a while back! I don't remember if it was the same play, *Our American Cousin*, or if he starred in another one then. At least Booth felt the same agony he inflicted on the President when he was hunted down and shot this week.

Poor Mrs. Lincoln, having her husband shot in the back of his head while sitting there watching a play! Although he lingered until morning, he never regained consciousness so they could exchange one last word or glance. I'm sure she worried whenever he traveled to the war fronts that something like this might happen. And then when they let their guard down . . .

In our area businesses closed and everyone draped their doors and windows with black crêpe for mourning. Even though Lincoln's funeral was the 19th at the White House, our Governor Crawford appointed April 23 as a day of fasting and prayer. Lawrence held a public service and funeral procession. We'll keep our vigil as Lincoln's body and his family slowly travel to Springfield, Illinois, for burial next week.

We pretended that the war was over, but its tragedy and gloom continue. Not all the Confederate troops have surrendered, so there are still skirmishes going on. Many of our neighbors have not come home yet, leaving many women to wonder about the fate of their loved ones. How long will it take for the nation to heal?

Instead of eagerly awaiting the birth of my first child, I mourn the loss of our President and all the others who have lost their lives during these past four years.

I wonder what life will be like for my child as it enters this world. Can I shelter it from the dangers it will face?

Mourning with the rest of the nation,

Maggie

Tuesday, May 16, 1865
Franklin, Kansas

Dear Caroline,

I have a baby boy! Marion Robert Pieratt was born last Tuesday, May 9, 1865.

I decided to wait with my letter until Lucinda delivered so I could tell you about both arrivals. You have another new nephew, Frank Hadley Kennedy, born yesterday to Lucinda and William James.

Although I haven't had much strength this past week, it feels good to sit outside in the sunshine to write this letter while my newborn is sleeping.

Goodness, I worried that the time would never come, then panicked when it did. James Monroe, my brave soldier, turned into a frantic deserter when my time came. It was Aunts Margaret and Polly who saw me through my first birth. I don't know how I would have done it without them. They moved in, talked me through the ordeal, and took care of both of us afterwards.

The two almost squabbled over the right way to do some tasks. Probably because of the way things are done differently in the North and South, or else because they have both hovered over me the past two weeks, and both wanted to be in charge.

Aunt Polly proudly wrapped Marion Robert in a new baby quilt she made for the occasion. Now I know where all my little scraps of material that were too small to use disappeared. Her nimble fingers transformed them into a miniature version of the Grandmother's Favorite. She had more patience that I would have had, and, I can tell by the excellent stitching, more experience.

You should have seen James Monroe beam when he first held his son. James checked out every finger and toe and declared his son perfect. He wanted the baby to carry on the name of his brother, Robert. I just hope he has a long and good life, unlike his uncle.

We have a planned celebration where I will show off our new son this weekend. James Monroe's sister, Sarah, is marrying David McCormick on Saturday. Her future husband is twice as old as she is, but in these times you hope they will be happy together for a very long time. There has been a rush of weddings ever since the men started arriving home. With the war officially over this month, many reunited couples can start their lives together now.

Think of all the new babies there will be next year! The Kennedys are doing their part with four births so far this year. We will keep Douglas County growing into the next generation!

Proud of our newest Kansan,

Maggie

Friday, June 16, 1865
Franklin, Kansas

Dear Caroline,

Thank you for your congratulatory letter and package. We received it June 8. The little shirt is just precious. Right now it is too big for Marion Robert, but he has grown so much in a month that I'm sure he'll soon be in it. He has so many hand-me-downs from his Kennedy cousins that I haven't bothered making many new things for him.

How are you? I hope all of you are well and having a productive summer. You mentioned being very busy with planting. Yes, it is good to have the menfolk back again on the farms. The newspaper said Kansas had the highest number of soldiers in the war of any state. Out of our population of 100,000, over 20,000 served some time during the four years. Three out of four families had someone involved in the fighting. Although many lives were lost, all are now back home in the state. We're noticing the farmsteads are being repaired and planted again, too.

Do you have many former soldiers moving into your area?

Thousands of new immigrants are pouring into Kansas. It has picked up since the last Confederates surrendered the first part of this month. They are coming in droves into Kansas to start a new life on the available homestead land. It seems like half the displaced population of the South, both black and white, are coming through here. Many soldiers are still in parts of their Union or Confederate uniforms, revolvers stuck in their belts. Most look like casualties of the war. Many don't have much to their names and are searching for a new start. They can't pick up their former lives because their farms, houses, and families don't exist anymore.

People here are trying to forget the past and get on with their lives, but it is natural to stay on guard. Promises of amnesty and protection induced most of the bushwhackers to surrender in the area, but one editor sarcastically commented that "horse stealing and robbery seems to be the most respectable mode of making a living just at the present time." Crime and violence by guerrillas and Jayhawkers are still rampant in some areas.

It certainly helped, though, that Quantrill died this month after being captured in Kentucky. Everyone was relieved that, as the newspaper quoted someone saying, "He was buried in a grave deep enough to keep him till the Judgment Day." Lets hope that the rest of the guerrillas meet their Maker and change their ways, one way or another.

Did Lucinda or William James write that they completed their move to Lawrence? The Williams Sawmill is being moved from Franklin to north of Lawrence, across the river into Jefferson County on the Mud Creek. Most of the lumber is depleted in the area around the mill, so they are moving it. William James is going to run it.

Franklin is rapidly dwindling as people and businesses abandon the town. Several of its houses were bought and moved to Lawrence after Quantrill burned the town, and Franklin never got back on its feet.

Other family news is that John Pieratt remarried on June 8 to a neighbor girl, Sarah Jane Wilkinson. The ceremony was held at William James's house. Since Sarah Jane is my age, I've known her from our school days. She is getting an instant family with the three Pieratt children still at home. The Pieratts have been through some difficult times in the last eleven years. I hope they have better times ahead.

Marion Robert is starting to stir, so I must close this letter before he starts fussing. Again, thank you for making something special for my first child.

Rocking my baby,

Maggie

Wednesday, August 9, 1865
Franklin, Kansas

Dear Caroline,

Greetings from the hot, dry state of Kansas. I hope you and your family are well. We're about to burn up with the temperature well over 100 degrees today. What I wouldn't give for a little rain to settle the dust and cool down the air.

Little Marion Robert has heat rash so bad that we are both miserable. I don't have any clothes on him today except for a diaper and cornstarch. I wouldn't ever do it, but wish I could dress the same in this heat.

Our drought continues with no hint of clouds to give us relief. Our wheat crop produced less than in the dismal year of 1860. Grasshoppers have worked on the stunted corn to the point we may not have a crop to harvest.

Gardening has been a challenge. I can't keep everything going in this heat, but I've been trying by hauling water to a different section of the garden every morning. By the time the searing afternoon sun hits its high point, the plants are limp again. Insects are invading the garden because it is the only green patch left on the place.

John Alonzo and Michael are considering moving down to Coffey County, Kansas. It about sixty miles southwest of here. They and Asa Dutton are looking at buying the Jinks and Taylor Sawmill operation that's along the Neosho River. Our brothers would probably rent or buy farmland in the area also. There is a big market for cattle, and the river bottomland there would yield lush grass for the animals. They have been over talking to James Monroe about moving with them. He and John Alonzo are the best of friends and would be good business partners. James Monroe is hesitant, saying that he just got this place going and doesn't want to sell yet.

I'm not sure he wants to leave his family. He and his siblings are close, and we'd be far enough away that they would only see one another a few times a year at the most.

I'd hate to leave my friends and Kennedy family here, but it would not be unbearable if our brothers were there. Before long they will settle down and marry, so I'll have sisters-in-law to keep me company. John said the town of Ottumwa near the sawmill is growing and would be a good place to raise a family. They have even started a college in town.

But if we follow the trail south to find new land to combine the Kennedy and Pieratt families, we would start over on virgin prairie again. James Monroe remembers the hard times his parents had when they moved to Kansas, and I don't think he wants to relive stark times. Our cousins have established farms in the Kennedy Valley and not interested in going either. Uncle Ned and Aunt Polly said they would go with us.

Personally, I'm tired of the strife that lurks in Douglas County and would like to strike out for a safer place. The last four years have made me independent enough to face the truth, so I'm not afraid. I've moved before and can do it again. Aunt Margaret says the "Kennedy fortitude" will carry me on if we decide to move.

James Monroe remembered his mother, Deborah, always did what was best for her family. Likewise, I must think of my son now. I'll let you know if we change our minds.

Tempted by new horizons,

Maggie

Friday, November 24, 1865
Franklin, Kansas

Dear Caroline,

I am in high spirits because of your last letter. It would be wonderful if you and Oliver move to Kansas next spring! You write that Mary Ann and Abraham are considering the move also? Just think, if Moses would leave Indiana, all of us brothers and sisters would be in the same state again. Wouldn't Mother be happy to know we were going to be together once more? I smile as I think of her now.

And we send Thanksgiving blessings to you. This year we have so many reasons to celebrate our holiday. We can be thankful that the war is over, the nation is starting to rebuild, and families are reunited this November.

Some people only see the problems of this last season's drought, but we know things have been worse—and will turn around again if we just hang on. Spring rains will sprout the seed and the cycle will start again. James Monroe and I will survive on our patch of prairie. We'll turn our land into rich farmland, multiply our produce and livestock, and make a name for ourselves.

The combination of our Kennedy and Pieratt families made a good union. Our mix of Northern and Southern views will balance, keeping us strong and alert to the perils of life.

Some of my unmarried friends wonder how I can be so optimistic. I tell them I look at the world through different eyes now. A husband and child changes all ideas of what is important in life. Motherhood gives you the courage of a lioness protecting her young. I will never let anything happen to my family if I can help it.

When I first arrived in the territory, Aunt Margaret told me I had to have more than a "stitch of courage" to survive on the plains of Kansas. I thought she was just making a play on words as she sat there quilting. But she had experienced troubles firsthand and was trying to prepare me for the rough life ahead. Now I know where our widowed aunt got her strength to move to

Kansas and withstand its first troubles. She did it for her children. Deborah Pieratt did the same for her family by carting them across the country. Only death robbed her of completing her task.

It must have torn our mother apart, knowing she was about to leave us. After having a child of my own, I realize it wasn't her choice to abandon me. I've come to better understand the sorrows of my past with the advent of Marion Robert's birth. I don't have dreams of abandonment any more. After all my years of private longing, I finally feel settled.

Strange how the birth of a tiny creature can change your life. I'm content now that I have a house and family. Kansas, with all its problems, is my home now, and will be for generations to come.

As I look up from my letter writing, my eyes travel to the old quilts lying on top of our bed. Earlier this evening I took these two out of my trunk to add to our bed for our increasingly cold nights. One was made by the Kennedy women, the other the Pieratt women. Stitched from scraps of clothing kept for sentimental reasons, they are reminders of the hands that made them, and I'm overwhelmed with memories of the women they represent.

I feel a sense of comfort as I realize how the quilts link us to their makers and to their dreams for us. Even though our mothers are gone, their love and strength are reflected in the stitches of these covers. Their trails of thread, in their quilts and in their journeys, link James Monroe and me together forever.

Tonight I'll feel secure wrapped in these quilts that traveled to Kansas. I hope you'll feel the same soon.

Pleasant dreams, dear sister.

Cherishing my home and family,

Maggie

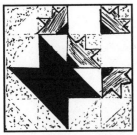

Basket of Lilies

Rocky Road to Kansas

Wild Goose Chase

Irish Puzzle

Stepping Stones

Eternal Triangle

Missouri Star

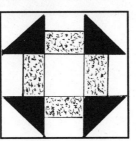

Churn Dash

Prairie Star

Union Star

Yankee Pride

Grandmother's Favorite

The James Monroe and Maggie Kennedy family-1873

Epilogue

The Civil War changed the lives of everyone in the nation. Here is a brief summary of the families featured in the *Trail of Thread* series and what they did after the war.

John Pieratt died of blood poisoning on November 5, 1868, at age fifty-one. His third wife, Sarah Jane, gave birth to his eleventh child, Jessie, two days later. All his surviving children married and stayed in Kansas except Emma, who moved to Texas but was buried in Kansas.

James and Mary Pieratt made it to California and settled in Sonoma County. The Tiptons stayed in Missouri.

Margaret Ralston Kennedy lived to be eighty-seven and to see her sixty-six grandchildren come into this world. Although she lost her daughter, Salina, in 1868, she was able to see the rest of her family prosper. Two of her sons, Joe and Tom, as well as her nephew, John Alonzo, served in the Kansas Legislature. Joe and Mary Kennedy established and presided over institutes for the deaf in Kansas for nine years and then moved to Colorado to start an institute in Colorado Springs.

Most of the Curlesses went back to Illinois right before the war, except Will and Nettie Curless, who moved to Barton County, Missouri, in 1867.

Maggie Pieratt's two sisters, Mary Ann Leonard and Caroline Perkins, and their families moved to Kansas in 1866. William James and Lucinda stayed in Lawrence. Her brothers, John Alonzo and Michael, moved to Ottumwa in Coffey County, Kansas, to farm and run a sawmill co-owned with Asa Dutton. Maggie and James Monroe followed them in 1867 and remained in the area for the rest of their lives.

Maggie had seven children. She lost two at early ages. John Alonzo Pieratt lived two months, and Mary Caroline Pieratt, a twin to Martha, died at age three on Maggie's thirty-fourth birthday.

Maggie died of typhoid fever on September 29, 1882, at age thirty-six. Her one-year-old baby, Asa Burton, died two days after from an overdose of medication.

In 1883 James Monroe Pieratt married his sister-in-law, Harriet Pieratt, widow of his brother, Belvard, and had two more daughters.

The Cleveland Tulip quilt mentioned in *Thimble of Soil* was given by Maggie Pieratt's daughter, Martha, to her great-niece (my mother), Letha Ione Akers, in 1938. The quilt was over a hundred years old at that time. It is still in her possession.

Family Charts

Michael B. Kennedy (1799-1847)
Hannah Rumery (1804-1850)

children:
1. **Moses Hopkins Kennedy** (1821-1878)
wife: **Margaret Sraufe** (1823-1878)
   1. Michael W. Kennedy (1846-1925)
   2. Thomas Lafayette Kennedy (1848-?)
   3. Adam Wilson Kennedy (1854-?)
   4. Simon Bartholomew Kennedy (1857-?)
   5. William Sidney Kennedy (1859-1950)

2. **Mary Ann Kennedy** (1825-1881)
1st husband: **Wilson J. Leonard** (1825-1852)
   1. Francis Marion Leonard (1846-?)
   2. Mahala Jane Leonard (1847-?)
   3. Amanda Leonard (1849-1851)
   4. George Wilson Leonard (1851-?)
2nd husband: **Abraham Liming** (1818-1881)
   1. Elizabeth Liming (1856-?)
   2. Jaspar Liming (1859-?)
   3. Warren Liming (1860-?)
   4. twin?- Walter Liming (1860-1860)
   5. Mary Ann Liming (1862-1919)
   6. Margaret Jane Liming (1866-?)

3. **no name Kennedy** stillborn (Jan 1828-1828)

4. **Sarah Thompson Kennedy** (Nov 1828-1849)
husband: John Leonard

5. **twin- Elizabeth H. Kennedy** (Nov 1828-?)

6. **no name Kennedy** stillborn (1831-1831)

7. **William James Kennedy** (1832-1903)
wife: **Lucinda Shields** (1839-1923)
    1. Alonzo Birk Kennedy (1858-1861)
    2. Mary Caroline Kennedy (1859-1861)
    3. Lizzie Jane Kennedy (1861-?)
    4. Asa Dutton Kennedy (1863-1953)
    5. Frank Hadley Kennedy (1865-1923)
    6. John Howard Kennedy (1867-?)
    7. Flora Martha Kennedy (1872-?)
    8. Horace Elwood Kennedy (1879-?)

8. **Michael Washington Kennedy** (1835-1900)
wife: **Catherine Crouse** (1850-1945)

9. **Hannah Caroline Kennedy** (1838-?)
husband: **Oliver P. Perkins** (1834-?)
    1. J. Bradford Perkins (1860-?)
    2. Edwin William Perkins (1862-?)
    3. Leander A. Perkins (1866-?)
    4. James Perkins (1868-?)
    5. John Perkins (1870-?)
    6. Lucinda Perkins (1874-?)

10. **John Alonzo Kennedy** (1841-1921)
1st wife: **Martha Mildred Strawn** (1849-1908)
    1. John William Kennedy (1870-1870)
    2. John Alonzo Kennedy Jr. (1872-1945)
    3. Harrison Lee Kennedy (1883-1928)
2nd wife: **Mary C. Williamson** (1853-1921)

11. **Margaret Jane "Maggie" Kennedy** (1846-1882)
husband: **James Monroe Pieratt** (1844-1913)
    1. Marion Robert Pieratt (1865-1933)
    2. John Alonzo Pieratt (1867-1867)
    3. James Monroe Pieratt Jr. (1870-1931)
    4. William Ira Pieratt (1873-1964)
    5. Martha Adeline Pieratt (1877-1948)
    6. twin- Mary Caroline Pieratt (1877-1880)
    7. Asa Burton Pieratt (1881-1882)

John Pieratt (1817-1868)
1st wife: Deborah Goodpaster (1821-1859)

children:
1. **Levi Pieratt** (1840-1840)

2. **Belvard Pieratt** (1841-1870)
1st wife: **Juliette Moore** (?-?)
2nd wife: **Harriet Catherine Jones** (1848-1932)
   1. Aetna May Pieratt (1869-1899)

3. **James Monroe Pieratt** (1844-1913)
1st wife: **Margaret Jane "Maggie" Kennedy** (1846-1882)
   see children under Kennedy
2nd wife: **Harriet Catherine Jones Pieratt** (1848-1932)
   1. Daisy Antonia Pieratt (1885-1983)
   2. Kate Hazel Pieratt (1874-1974)

4. **Robert Letcher Pieratt** (1846-1863)

5. **Sarah Pieratt** (1848-1903)
husband: **David Titus McCormick** (1832-1906)
   1. Charles McCormick (1866-1878)
   2. Mary Darling McCormick (1868-1874)
   3. Jettie Belle McCormick (1870-1888)
   4. Franklin McCormick (1873-?)
   5. John William McCormick (1878-1880)
   6. Dolly McCormick (1881-?)

6. **George Ann Pieratt** (1850-1879)
husband: **Reuben Frances Moore** (1840-?)
   1. Thomas Moore (1866-1874)
   2. Johnnie Moore (1868-?)
   3. Albert Moore (1870-?)
   4. Rupert Eastmere Moore (1872-?)
   5. Sarah "Sadie" Bell Moore (1874-1942)
   6. Helen Moore (1876-?)
   7. Margaret "Maggie" May Moore (1877-?)
   8. Clementine Moore (1879-?)

7. **Emma Pieratt** (1853-1929)
husband: **Isaac Bentley** (1844-1914)
   1. Jessie Belle Bentley (1869-?)
   2. Maude Bentley (1875-1938)
   3. Bert Bentley (?-?)

8. **John Franklin Pieratt** (1855-1908)
wife: **Sarah Elizabeth Samuels** (1860-1929)
   1. Sarah Edna Pieratt (1877-1959)
   2. Mary Ellen Pieratt (1879-1921)
   3. Bertha Margaret Pieratt (1882-1951)
   4. John Franklin Pieratt, Jr. (1883-1960)
   5. James William Pieratt (1885-1946)
   6. Emma Kate Pieratt (1889-1926)
   7. Dolly Patience Pieratt (1895-?)
   8. Nellie Marie Pieratt (1902-?)

John's 2nd wife: **Nancy Shields (1830-1863)**

children:
 9. **Joseph Pieratt** (1860-1860)

10. **Mary Pieratt** (1861-?)
husband: **George Washington Gluyas** (?-?)
   1. Chalmers Gluyas (1880-1880)
   2. Archie Gluyas (1881-1881)
   3. Edwin Gluyas (1886-1886)
   4. Luella Maude Gluyas (1887-1892)
   5. Arthur Carl Gluyas (1888-?)
   6. Angel Gladys Gluyas (1892-1892)
   7. Myron Gluyas (1895-?)
   8. Maybell Irene Gluyas (1901-?)

John's 3rd wife: **Sarah Jane Wilkerson (1846-1914)**

children:
11. **William Graham Pieratt** (1866-1933)
wife: Lydia A. Tyler (1868-1940)
   1. James Lewis Pieratt (1890-1971)
   2. Agnes L. Pieratt (1893-?)

3. William Earl Pieratt (1895-?)
4. Charles A. Pieratt (1897-1968)
5. May Pieratt (1900-?)
6. Mary Jane Pieratt (1904-1982)
7. Stella? Bertha? Pieratt (?-?)

12. **Jesse Pieratt** (1868-1951)
wife: Eva Francis Hines (1870-1943)
1. Matilda Jane Pieratt (1890-1953)

Joseph Shields (1811-1883)
1st wife: Mary McLaren (1810-1879)

children:
1. **Nancy Shields** (1830-1863)
husband: **John Pieratt** (1817-1868)
see children under Pieratt

2. **Jane Shields** (1832-1897)
husband: **Joseph Weaver Hopping** (1822-1880)

3. **Robert Fulton Shields** (1833-1864)
wife: **Margaret Seaton ?** (?-?)

4. **Benjamin Shields** (1835-1904)
wife: **Mary A. Abbott** (?-?)

5. **Elizabeth Shields** (1837-?)
husband: **? Pennington** (?-?)

6. **Lucinda Shields** (1839-1923)
husband: **William James Kennedy** (1832-1903)
  see children under Kennedy

7. **Martha Shields** (1841-?)
husband: **John Francis Roberts** (1830-1926)

8. **William Shields** (1843-?)
wife: **Millie Ann Abbott** (?-?)

9. **Rachel A. Shields** (1845-1900)

10. **Kinsey Shields** (1848-1848)

11. **Amaziah Howard Shields** (1850-1893)

Joseph's second wife: **Rachel S. Wilkinson (1831-1901)**

Hugh Kennedy (1796-1845)
Margaret Jane Ralston (1800-1887)

children:
1. **Elizabeth A. Kennedy** (1821-1853)
husband: **Abraham Liming** (1818-1881)
   1. Raymond Liming (1842-?)
   2. Virginia A. Liming (1844-?)
   3. Amanda J. Liming (1846-?)
   4. George N. Liming (1849-?)
   5. Matilda Liming (1852-?)

2. **William Bainbridge "Bridge" Kennedy** (1822-1887)
wife: **Elizabeth Jane Curless** (1829-1916)
   1. Margaret Jane Kennedy (1848-1849)
   2. Eugene Marshall Kennedy (1850-1923)
   3. Flora Martha Kennedy (1853-1886)
   4. Oscar Curless Kennedy (1855-1922)
   5. Josephine Kennedy (1857-1858)
   6. Ella Alice Kennedy (1860-1929)
   7. Lillie May Kennedy (1863-1928)
   8. Harvey Elmer Kennedy (1865-1865)
   9. Lucy Lena Kennedy (1867-1942)
   10. Effie Gertrude Kennedy (1871-?)

3. **Jonathan Ralston "Joe" Kennedy** (1824-1883)
1st wife: **Mary E. Neal** (1833-?)
   1. Oliver Jeff Kennedy (1851-1918)
2nd wife: **Mary E. Jones** (? - ?)
   2. Matilda Kennedy (1854-?)
   3. Emma Kennedy (1855-1929)
   4. Katherine Kennedy (1857-?)
   5. Oran J. Kennedy (1859-?)

4. **Sarah Jane "Sed" Kennedy** (1826-1902)
husband: **John Neal** (1801- 1883)
   1. Charles E. Neal (1856-1927)
   2. Bainbridge Neal (1860-?)

3. Jesse Bell Neal (1862-?)
4. Randolph Neal (1868-?)

5. **Zanetta Olivia "Nettie" Kennedy** (1828-1911)
husband: **William H. Curless** (1827-1909)
   1. Joseph Warren Curless (1849-1913)
   2. Sarah Catherine Curless (1851-?)
   3. Frank Gilbert Curless (1853-1941)
   4. Augusta Jane Curless (1855-1939)
   5. Josephine Curless (1858-?)
   6. Mary Curless (1860-?)
   7. George Benson Curless (1863-1940)
   8. Ella Alice "Nellie" Curless (1865-1949)
   9. Charles Van Pelt Curless (1868-1951)
  10. Edmund K. Curless (1871-1931)

6. **Catherine Blackburn "Cate" Kennedy** (1830-1909)
husband: **Collins Holloway** (1832-1905)
   1. Rose D. Holloway (1852-1944)
   2. Emery A. Holloway (1856-?)
   3. Dora L. Holloway (1860-1936)
   4. Scott R. Holloway (1862-1946)
   5. Grant W. Holloway (1864-1902)
   6. Margaret D. Holloway (1866-1946)
   7. Thomas Kennedy Holloway (1869-1954)

7. **Oliver Perry "Scott" Kennedy** (1831-1917)
1st wife: **Louise Price** (? -?)
   1. Jennie L. Kennedy (1855-1927)
2nd wife: **Martha M. Woodruff** (1842-1922)
   2. Frank R. Kennedy (1862-1932)
   3. Lizzie Belle Kennedy (1863-1944)
   4. Melinda Kennedy (1867-1928)
   5. Margaret M. "Mollie" Kennedy (1871-1964)
   6. Fred J. Kennedy (1875-?)

8. **Thomas Hamer "Major" Kennedy** (1832-1890)
wife: **Martha E. Nolan** (1841-1877)
   1. Thomas Hugh Kennedy (1861-1919)
   2. Martha Belle Kennedy (1862-?)

3. Walter C. Kennedy (1866-?)
4. Charles Kennedy (?-?)

9. **Leander Jackson "Doc" Kennedy** (1835-1903)
wife: **Amanda Ellen Todd** (1841-1926)
   1. Isabelle Kennedy (1860-1860)
   2. Eva Lynn Kennedy (1861-1947)
   3. Elmer Hugh Kennedy (1863-1929)
   4. Charles Todd Kennedy (1866-1950)
   5. Harvey Leander Kennedy (1868-1937)
   6. Ida May Kennedy (1871-1873)
   7. Clarence Liming Kennedy (1874-?)
   8. Albert Rutherford Kennedy (1876-1969)
   9. Harry Ansil Kennedy (1881-1923)

10. **Joseph Warren Kennedy** (1837-1838)

11. **Mary Ann Kennedy** (1839-1839)

12. **Matilda M. Kennedy** (1840-1852)

13. **Salina F. Kennedy** (1841-1868)
husband: **Alonzo Hindman** (1840-1914)
   1. Charles Hindman (1860-?)
   2. Capitola Hindman (1862-?)
   3. Arthur Hindman (1864-?)
   4. Harry Hindman (1866-?)
   5. baby Hindman (1868-1868)

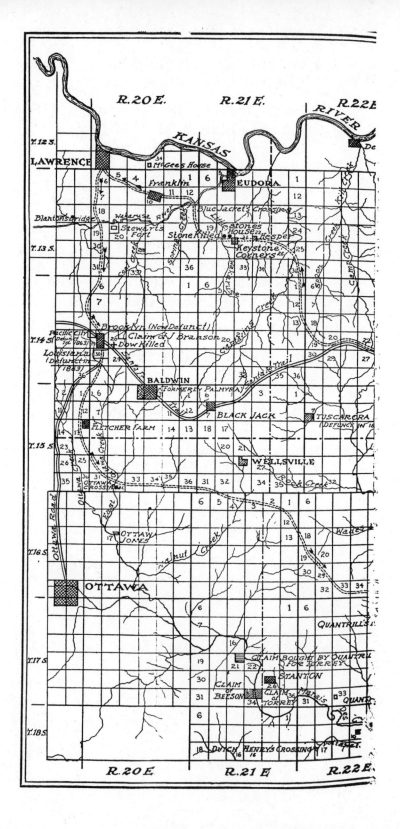

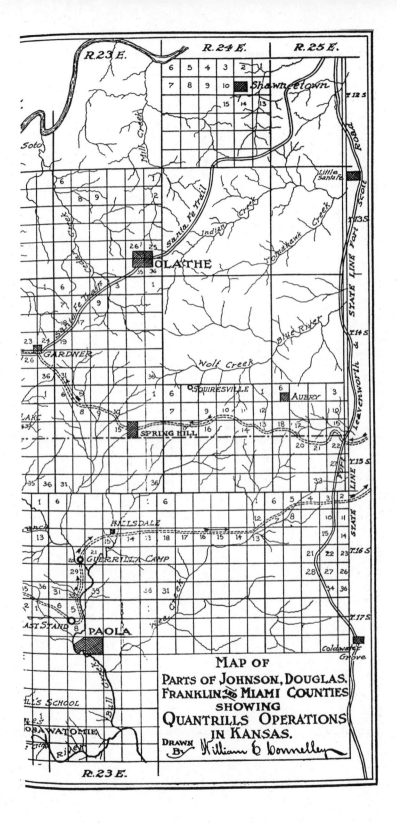

MAP OF
PARTS OF JOHNSON, DOUGLAS,
FRANKLIN AND MIAMI COUNTIES
SHOWING
QUANTRILL'S OPERATIONS
IN KANSAS.

DRAWN BY William E Connelley

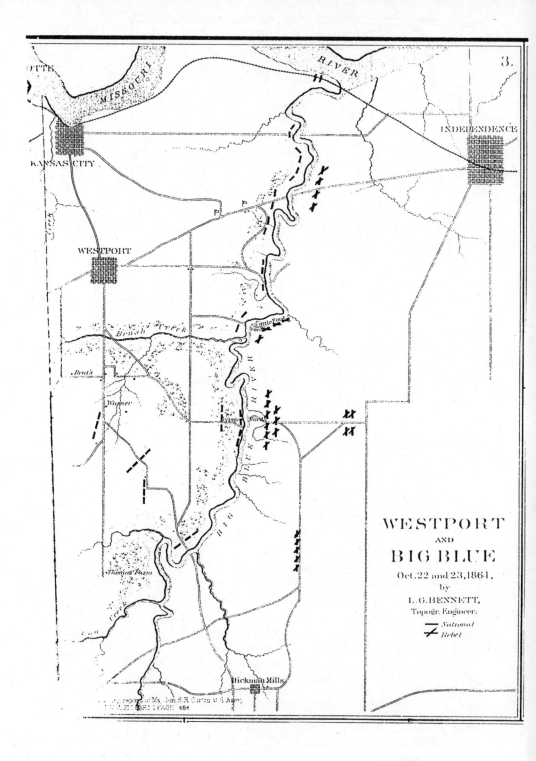

WESTPORT
AND
BIG BLUE
Oct. 22 and 23, 1864,
by
L. G. BENNETT,
Topogr. Engineer.

National
Rebel

Selected Bibliography

Abel, Annie Heloise. *The American Indian as Participant in the Civil War*. Cleveland: The Arthur H. Clar Company, 1919.

Andreas, A. T. *History of the State of Kansas*. Chicago, Ill.: A. T. Andreas, 1883.

Angle, Paul M. *A Pictorial History of the Civil War Years*. Garden City, New York: Doubleday & Company, Inc., 1980.

Atherly, Mary Lou De Long. *Angie Lives: Historical Sketches of Families from the Strawn, Kansas Area*. 1988.

———. *Yesterday's Tomorrow: A History of Strawn, Kansas and Surrounding Territory*. 1982.

Billings, John D. *Hartack and Coffee or The Unwritten Story of Army Life*. Boston: George M Smith & Co., 1887.

Boardman, Fon W. Jr., *America and the Civil War Era 1850-1875*. New York: Henry Z. Walck, Inc., 1976.

Brackman, Barbara, Jennie A. Chinn, Gayle R. Davis, Terry Thompson, Sara Reimer Farley, and Nancy Hornback. *Kansas Quilts & Quilters*. Lawrence: University Press of Kansas, 1993.

Britton, Wiley. *Civil War on the Border Vol I and II*. New York: G. P. Putnam's Sons, 1899.

———. *Memoirs of the Rebellion on the Border, 1863*. Chicago: Cushing, Thomas & Co. Publishers, 1882.

———. *The Union Indian Brigade in the Civil War*. Reprint. Ottawa, Kan.: Kansas Heritage Press, 1992.

Brownlee, Richard S. *Gray Ghosts of the Confederacy: Guerrilla Warfare in the West 1861-1865*. Baton Rouge: Louisiana State University Press, 1958.

Castel, Albert. *A Frontier State of War: Kansas 1861-1865*. Lawrence, Kan.: Kansas Heritage Press, 1992.

Colton, Ray C. *The Civil War in the Western Territories*. Norman: University of Oklahoma Press, 1985.

Connelley, William Elsey. *Quantrill and the Border Wars*. Cedar Rapids, Iowa: The Torch Press, 1910.

Cross, Helen Reeder. *Life in Lincoln's America*. New York: Random House, Inc.,1964.

Douglas County Genealogical Society, Inc. *Complete Tombstone Census of Douglas County, Kansas, Volume 2*. Lawrence, Kan., 1989.

Eakin, Joanne Chiles. *Tears and Turmoil: Order #11*. Independence, Missouri, 1996.

Frost, Lawrence A. *General Custer's Libbie*. Seattle: Superior Publishing Company, 1976.

Gleed, Charles S., ed. *The Kansas Memorial: A Report of the Old Settlers' Meetings held at Bismarck Grove, Kansas, September 15 and 16, 1879*. Kansas City, Mo.: Press of Ramsey, Millett and Hudson, 1880.

Goodrich, Thomas. *Black Flag: Guerrilla Warfare on the Western Border, 1861-1865*. Bloomington: Indiana University Press, 1995.

―――. *Bloody Dawn: The Story of the Lawrence Massacre*. Kent, Ohio: Kent State University Press, 1991.

Gragg, Rod. *The Civil War Quiz and Fact Book*. New York: Harper & Row, Publishers, 1985.

Hall, Carrie A., and Rose G. Kretsinger. *The Romance of the Patchwork Quilt in America*. Caldwell, Idaho: The Caxton Printers, Ltd., 1935.

Josephy, Alvin M. Jr. *The Civil War in the American West*. New York: Alfred A. Knopf, Inc., 1991.

Kansas State Journal, newspaper issues from 1861-1865.

Kinsley, D. A. *Favor the Bold. Custer: The Civil War Years.* New York: Holt, Rinehart and Winston, Inc., 1968.

Litter, Loren K. *Bleeding Kansas: The Border War in Douglas and Adjacent Counties.* Baldwin City, Kan.: Champion Publishing, 1987.

———. *William Clarke Quantrill: The Man who Burned Lawrence.* Baldwin City, Kan.: Champion Publishing, 1987.

Mettger, Zak. *Till Victory is Won: Black Soldiers in the Civil War.* New York: Lodestar Books, 1994.

Mitchell, Patricia B. *Confederate Camp Cooking.* Chatham, Va.: Patricia B. Mitchell Foodways Publications, 1991.

———. *Union Army Camp Cooking.* Chatham, Virg.: Patricia B. Mitchell Foodways Publications, 1991.

Rawley, James A. *Race and Politics: "Bleeding Kansas" and the Coming of the Civil War.* Philadelphia: J. B. Lippincott Company, 1969.

Reynolds, Arlene. *The Civil War Memories of Elizabeth Bacon Custer.* Austin: University of Texas Press, 1994.

Schwartz, Gerald, ed. *A Woman Doctor's Civil War: Esther Hill Hawks' Diary.* Columbia: University of South Carolina, 1989.

Shea, John C. *Reminiscences of Quantrell's [sic] Raid upon the City of Lawrence, Kas.* Kansas City, Mo., 1879.

Smith, Elbert B. *The Death of Slavery: The United States, 1837-65.* Chicago: The University of Chicago Press, 1967.

Steele, Phillip W., and Steve Cottrell. *Civil War in the Ozarks.* Gretna, La.: Pelican Publishing Co., 1993.

Straubing, Harold Elk. *In Hospital and Camp: The Civil War through the Eyes of Its Doctors and Nurses.* Harrisburg, Pa.: Stackpole Books, 1993.

Sullivan, Marge Nichols, ed. *My Folks and the Civil War.* Topeka, Kan.: Capper Press, 1994.

White, Anne Terry. *North to Liberty: The Story of the Underground Railroad.* Champaign, Ill.: Garrard Publishing Co., 1972.

About the Author

Linda K. Hubalek

A door may close in your life but a window will open instead.

Linda Hubalek knew years ago she wanted to write a book someday about her great-grandmother, Kizzie Pieratt, but it took a major move in her life to point her toward her new career in writing.

Hubalek's chance came unexpectedly when her husband was transferred from his job in the Midwest to the West Coast. She had to sell her wholesale floral business and find a new career.

Homesick for her family and the farmland of the Midwest, she turned to writing about what she missed, and the inspiration was kindled thus to write about her ancestors and the land they homesteaded.

What resulted was the *Butter in the Well* series, four books based on the Swedish immigrant woman who homesteaded the family farm in Kansas where Hubalek grew up.

In her second series, *Trail of Thread*, Hubalek follows her maternal ancestors who travel to Kansas in the 1850s. These three books relive the turbulent times the pioneer women faced before and during the Civil War.

Linda Hubalek lives in the Midwest again, close to the roots that started her writing career.

The author loves to hear from her readers. You may write to her in care of Book Kansas!/Butterfield Books, PO Box 407, Lindsborg, KS 67456.